DEATH
OF A
SOLDIER

DEATH
OF A
SOLDIER

A MOTHER'S STORY

MARGARET EVISON

Biteback Publishing

First published in Great Britain in 2012 by
Biteback Publishing Ltd
Westminster Tower
3 Albert Embankment
London SE1 7SP
Copyright © Margaret Evison 2012

ISBN 978-1-84954-449-8

10 9 8 7 6 5 4 3 2 1

A CIP catalogue record for this book is available from the British Library.

Set in Caslon
Cover design by Namkwan Cho

Printed and bound in Great Britain by
CPI Group (UK) Ltd, Croydon CR0 4YY

To Elizabeth

CONTENTS

ACKNOWLEDGEMENTS

With very many thanks to my publisher Biteback and my literary agent Lizzy Kremer, both of whom took on a risky elderly unknown with little to protect them. John knows how much I have appreciated his patience and good sense, but here it is in print. I owe much to some who have given their support and considerable time, particularly John MacAuslen, Professor Richard Robinson, Anthony Temple QC, Dr Tom Stevens, Mick Brown and Charles Moore. It is hard to find words to express my appreciation of the kindness of friends who have read drafts and the support of Colonel Tom Bonas.

GLOSSARY

1 WG	1st Battalion Welsh Guards
3 PARA	Guards Parachute Platoon
Adjt	Adjutant
AH	Apache attack helicopter
Ak-47s	assault rifles
ANA	Afghan National Army
AO	area of operation
AT	adventure training
BATUS	British Army Training Unit Suffield, Canada
BVM	bag valve mask
Callsign	a name or number assigned to each unit for radio/battlefield identification purposes
Callsign going firm	to stop/go static, usually whilst scanning the ground ahead or to take stock, check equipment or send a report
CASEVAC	casualty evacuation helicopter
CAT	combat action tourniquet
CLP	combat logistic patrol
Comd Offr BG	Commanding Officer Battlegroup
Command 2 i/c	Company Second in Command

CP	command post
ECM	electronic counter measure
FAM	fighting age male
FFD	first field dressing
FOB	forward operating base
FST	Fire Support Team
Gdsm	Guardsman
GMG	grenade machine gun
Gnr	Gunner
HEMCON	haemostatic dressing
HESCO	multi-cellular defence walls
Icom	radio system/scanner
IED	improvised explosive device
INS	insurgents
IO	Intelligence Officer
ISAF	International Security Assistance Force
ITT	Interpreter
JHF	Joint Helicopter Force
LBdr	Lance Bombadier
LCpl	Lance Corporal
LN	local national
LSgt	Lance Sergeant
LtCol	Lieutenant Colonel
M-16s	rifle
MASTIFFS	Army patrol vehicle
MERT	Medical Emergency Response Team
MFC	Mortar Fire Controller
MOD	Ministry of Defence

Multiple	group of soldiers
NCO	Non-Commissioned Officer
OC	Officer in Charge
OMLT	Operational Mentor and Liaison Team
Ops Offr	Operations Officer
Osprey	body armour
PB	patrol base
PCD	Platoon Commanders Division
PKM	PK machine gun
R & R	rest and recuperation leave
RAMC	Royal Army Medical Corps
RPGs	rocket propelled grenades
RSOI	Reception, Staging, and Onward Integration
SAF	small arms fire
Sangars	sandbag fortifications
SAS	Special Air Service
Shura	consultation, meeting
SIB	Special Investigation Branch
Stag	duty
TA	Territorial Army
TFH	Task Force Helmand
TIC	troops in combat
UBACS	under body armour combat shirt
UK SF	Special Forces
VHF	Very High Frequency radio

FOREWORD

The death of a young soldier is always sad. We all
know that. But, luckily, few of us experience it
directly. Few of us know what it feels like for the people
who loved the dead man most. And although we all have
compassion for the bereaved, there is a sense in which we
do not quite wish to know. We want to turn away from
something so painful.

Margaret Evison's son, Mark, a lieutenant in the Welsh
Guards, was killed fighting in Afghanistan. This book
tells us what happened. It also deals with all the thoughts
that naturally flow from such a terrible event. Should he
ever have gone? Could his life have been saved? Was the
British presence in Afghanistan pointless? Is war itself
ever justified?

No one can answer all these questions with absolute
authority, but one of the great merits of this book is that it
shows how a mother finds herself asking them. It sets out
the shock of her loss and the pattern of her grief. It is very
rationally written, which makes it all the more powerful
when it deals with feelings that are too deep for reason.

As Margaret explains, I met her when we travelled together to Afghanistan in 2010, she hoping to learn something from seeing the country in which Mark died. She includes her observations from that visit in this book. It struck me at once how brave Margaret was: Afghanistan is a difficult country for any traveller, for a woman particularly so. For her it must have been almost unbearable. But she bore it with courage so that she could make more sense of the story in which she found herself caught up.

Having seen some of the country and experienced war death as a mother, she is in a powerful position to write about it and its consequences. This is a remarkable work, moving from the personal to the wider picture and addressing aspects of national interest.

Margaret wanted to do justice and honour to the son she loved. She has succeeded. I never met Mark, but the reader can discover him, vividly recorded, in this book – extrovert, courageous, handsome, but also, as good soldiers quietly are, sensitive. Mark is dead, but his mother has brought him alive.

Charles Moore
October 2012

CHAPTER ONE

'THE REST IS SILENCE.'

This is the story of a journey, a journey not through the awesome vistas of great mountains and wild grey seas but a more perilous journey, through the love one has for others, the intensities of care and compassion we feel for each other, and the structures we humans have built to protect ourselves from those great heights and depths. I understand more completely now that when there is love there will also be pain and suffering.

It is a journey through despair, but also a tale of surprises, sometimes magical. I am telling it partly because I have to – to lick a deep wound, crying as I write. But also because when one travels to a new world one wants to tell about it. And to pay my respects to a young man who commanded such love and respect in his short life. Then it was over. In the words on his gravestone, 'A man of great courage, compassion, distinction and charm. Farewell great heart.'

Mark's death was one of many, both in this conflict and in others – old war cemeteries speak of these. But for me at the time it was the only death.

His was the path of an ordinary person who tried to do his best and who cared intensely about his men, soldiers in Afghanistan. Those childhood years of shaping, cajoling, encouraging him to be responsible finally bore fruit. It ended as it always does, with those left behind trying to understand and make some sense of it. Many people tried to help with his loss in their own way, often powerfully with their almost inexplicable kindness. But surprisingly I found that the great institutions of state, politics and law were the smallest of all when it came to allowing understanding and the simple sensitivities of human life. Death is much bigger than any of us, but these institutions box it up as office routine.

Where does the journey begin? There are many places, many markers. At its most prosaic, it should be the April leaves around the front door, the brief kiss, the perfunctory 'See you in six months.' As son and mother we were bound by deep mutual care, both hoping to make it easier for the other. I wanted it to be an ordinary farewell, the sort that assumes a return. I did not want to entice the silent devils waiting in the wings by naming them, giving them a voice or any power at all. I did not want him to have to carry any of my worry; he had enough himself. He had chosen this – his beloved Welsh Guards, his Army – and I wanted to do my bit, supporting him, downplaying my own fears. I gave him a hug, an extra squeeze.

We had had the few days of Easter together; Mark,

his sister Elizabeth, their partners and my partner John, doing what families do best: playing games, eating and drinking, having fun. The weekend felt all-important, full-blown and extroverted, but now the tight goodbye was hiding so much.

During the weekend we had time to walk together down the garden and we discussed death, that most distant and forbidden subject for young people as they embrace life. I wanted to help him with it, partly so that he could help his men with their grief if he had to, and also so that he could deal with his own. I did not think about mine. I told him that the process of dying was not difficult, that consciousness and awareness and the sense of oneself were protected by a thick membrane of dullness when one's body was struggling. People who know they will die adjust to it and accept it. He told me he was worried that he might make a mistake and cause the death of another. He did not discuss the possibility of his own death.

Immediately after that Easter weekend, on 13 April 2009, he went away to his other world of soldiering. He had been cautious about telling me exactly the dangers of where he was going, underplaying them, or perhaps he did not know. Much later I understood what a challenge it had been. He emailed occasionally, tried to ring once but the line was dead in seconds, and wrote three times, in easy language that would not worry. His letter sent on 28 April read:

Sorry we were unable to speak properly a couple of nights ago. The phone has very bad reception where we are and we also do not have a charger and so now it has run out of battery we have no way of charging it …

Things here are great. We have now settled into the fort and are awaiting ten Afghan National Army bods as well as an interpreter before we can patrol to our full extent.

The poppy harvest is still ongoing but coming to a close and the fighting season is supposedly about to start, could be interesting for a few weeks.

We have bought a turkey off a local farmer and he will be included on the BBQ on Sunday night which will be my first fresh meat in two weeks. On top of that next Sunday is my shower day and so double-whammy. Can't wait. It's funny how the smallest things like a shower you really miss when it is not on tap.

I was so keen for contact, for a little reassurance that my world and his were still touching, overlapping. I sent him weekly parcels, the silly things that mothers send: custard, suntan lotion, cake, sweets, noodles, bits of his childhood to make him know that his mother was still there. Finally, in early May, before I left the house around 8 a.m. there he was on the telephone telling me how it was, hesitant and jumbled sentences as we both tried to ask all the right questions and get all the answers. He wrote about that call in his diary later that day, regretting that he may have worried me by being too honest, taking the mute button off.

Then another significant day three days after that call, beginning as a beautiful May morning. There was a profound feeling of wellbeing about the day. The garden was restless with bloom as it had been many Mays before, in its own tart green, shy, pretty and exhilarated way. An annual community party the evening before, jovial with old friends, had left a sense of life stretching behind and ahead. There was calm, peace, Saturday morning pleasures and slow busyness. I had been to get the paper from the local shop and as I turned into the drive I saw a casually dressed man apparently loitering with some intent, talking to a neighbour as he did so.

'Can I help?' I asked.

He said he was a major in the Army.

'I have a son in the Army.'

'I know. Would you mind if we went inside to speak?'

As we walked down the path I said I hoped nothing was wrong, but he was non-committal. We went into my back room, the seven large angled windows overlooking the garden. He introduced himself, Major Ransom, he was a casualty notifications officer. He said that Mark had been shot, very seriously injured. He explained the three categories of injury: very, very serious (fatal); very serious; and serious. He could tell me nothing more, except that Mark was priority one to be flown back to England, and that I would have a visiting officer to help me who would come later in the day. I have no memory of Major Ransom going but I do not think he was there for long.

It is hard to describe what I felt. Unreality is the best word. There was no information, so I fell back on my experience of treatable rugby wounds, old optimism and then magical thinking about two arms, two lungs and the wonders of medicine and of healing. I felt helpless, there was no guidance here – what should I do? Should I ask Mark to be brought to the large London teaching hospital where I worked so that he was near home, arrange help from surgeons I knew; should I try to go to Afghanistan? I could not get hold of my daughter Elizabeth, out enjoying the day in south London somewhere, nor my ex-husband David, living in Berlin. I rang a GP friend, and her medical husband with his Army connections visited on his bicycle ride. He spoke of the excellent medical resources in Bastion Hospital, Helmand province, a unit which he had visited and where Mark would be.

I did as I always do for relief: I took to gardening, the gentle rituals of creation. The garden had been my solace before during difficult times – for many months after David left, during work trials. Mark loved it, and had laid the lawn with a friend, keen for some extra money to pay for extra fun. The lawn was now so green and soft around the comfort of large, timeless trees. Nature throbbing all around, pushing to survive. Now, once again, I was calmed by its young energy and yet its peace, its patterns. Sadly, for several years afterwards an early May garden would evoke the same foreboding, of what?

Strangely I continued to be optimistic. It may be my nature; most likely it was our past together. Mark had failed to thrive as a baby and although those first days were long ago and far from my mind, it may have for ever marked me. His early life had been a struggle, but in the end, six years later, he was fine. From shaky beginnings we were both survivors. It would be so this time too, but still I wanted to look after him.

Later that afternoon, my Ministry of Defence visiting officer Steve arrived – a stocky, straightforward, giving man. He wanted to do his best here. And he did, because of his confident and translucent openness. He said he would be at my side for several months if I needed him, and in the weeks to come he was indeed happy to come at any time, negotiating the family tensions that slowly grew with the pain, and giving me information as he had it. He said that he had nearly died in a ditch in Iraq and now here he was. He liked his cup of tea and chided me for not feeding the cat, which meowed assertively for food to any new visitor. But even he could not tell me what Mark's injuries actually were.

I found Elizabeth later in the day, and she and her partner came down. I have little memory of telling them what had happened, perhaps there was too little to tell. Mark's father David remained in Berlin. I reassured him:

Mark would be injured and in hospital, why did he not come towards the end of the week to spend a few days alone with him? We both believed my reassurance.

The weekend slowly moved along. No more information, except that Mark was stable and on life support in Bastion Hospital. But he did not come home. Then I heard that he had been shot in the shoulder and would come back when they could bring him. It was a day later when I realised: even though he was priority one he was still not here, and I knew then that he must be fighting for his life. Early that Sunday morning was almost the time his body gave up and his pupils finally dilated, and the doctors gave up hope also. I did not know that until much later.

I was told that Sunday that Mark had injured the subclavian artery of his right arm. There was a suggestion of internal damage, perhaps lungs and liver, but nothing concrete. I printed off pages from the internet about the subclavian artery, a large important artery in his shoulder feeding his arm, and wondered if his injuries would be too serious to allow him a life, or if his life could be lived without an arm, damaged for ever. All communication with Bastion, in and out, had been blanked by the Army, as happens when someone dies. Was this because of Mark, I wondered? I had not heard of any other injured or dying soldiers.

Finally, late that afternoon, I was told that he was to be flown back to Selly Oak Hospital in Birmingham, an

NHS hospital that has trauma facilities and expertise in treating injured soldiers. The flight would involve three aircraft and two changes from one to the other, as he was carried from Bastion to Kandahar to London and Birmingham. He could die at any point. If he died in transit I would be informed and he would be taken back to Bastion.

Elizabeth and I drove to Birmingham in the evening, mentally ticking off the plane changes as the mobile phone remained silent. We stayed in a tatty bed and breakfast near the hospital with dark rooms and cheap, flowered wallpaper, run by a grumpy man. I hardly slept, restless with uncertainty and the unfamiliarity of the unpleasant surroundings. It was a dreadful night; the only comfort was Elizabeth sleeping next to me. I was desperate to see Mark – I wanted both my children with me.

Steve picked us up on Monday to take us to Selly Oak Hospital. We left the house too early for breakfast, rumpled and tired. As we walked across the lawns an ambulance went past – that was Mark, I was told, because it had a police escort. He would have to be settled in first, linked up to machines, and then I could see him with the consultant. I was in a hurry, frustrated. I was first taken to the family's sleeping quarters and introduced to Oona, a large comforting Territorial Army nurse who seemed to understand and would be looking after us.

Then we were allowed to visit Mark. My job had

prepared me for the red-brick efficiency of sprawling buildings, long corridors and then intensive care, all quietly efficient with soulless hooked-up beds. I knew this world – it was usually comfortable to me. Mark had a room on one side of the ward; the family was given a sitting room nearby to use for the next two days.

The consultant was stuffy and formal, doing his job to explain, forgetting that I came from a medical world. Elizabeth sat with me, then left, unable to stay. He said that there was only a very small chance that Mark was not brain dead, that at present his body was slowed by large amounts of pain medication and that they would have to withdraw this, and then carry out brain stem tests the next day to see if there was any response. He explained that the brain stem – the conduit to the brain, the messaging – was probably gone, and that the chance of recovery was very small. He said it would be unfair to Mark if we left him on life support machines, as he would deteriorate but not wake up. I was aware of a huge thirst as he spoke, wanting many glasses of water. In the day-to-day busyness of intensive care there was no space for feeling and sentiment, if there was any to be had. I felt drained, empty of life, still clinging to that small chance, unable to accept death.

There was Mark with his beautiful brown lithe body, his sunburnt feet strapped with flip-flop marks, his handsome broad-boned face, peaceful and asleep. This was my Markie, the Mark I knew, despite the tubes and the huge wound in his side, apparently raw flesh taped over with see-through dressing, and his swollen right arm high in a solid plastic sling. I wanted to take him home. I spent much time with him talking, whispering, touching him, stroking his hair, holding him, willing him to wake. I did not understand then why he slept. I visited again and again, wanting more and unable to accept less, knowing that this might be the last time, but not understanding that it would be for ever.

Mark had come with a hospital diary filled in by the nursing staff at Bastion Hospital, which I read.

09/05/09, 17.00: Mark, my name is Karen, I'm a TA Nursing Major. I've been with you since you came into intensive care at 13.00 hours. Everyone has been doing everything possible to help you recover. Stuart, the lad injured with you, is rooting for you. I've been to see him. Padre Morgan from the Welsh Guards has been to see you and the hospital Padre, Nicola (a Welsh lass), said a blessing for you. You are in theatre for the second time at this moment. Plans are being made to get you back to the UK, the RAF have confirmed that the critical care support team have been mobilised, so are on their way soon.

20.30: Mark, you're back from theatre, several of the hospital staff have given you their blood, as you've used up the hospital supply! The pharmacist gave you his platelets, he's Estonian – says they're good quality as Estonia makes good beer. You have had 30+ units of blood, 30+ units of plasma. 3 doses factor 7 @ £7,000 each. So I can quote your service number and hospital no. I've checked it so many times today. Karen X

09/05/09, 20.55: Hi Mark, I'm Maggie Durant, the senior nurse for the hospital. I was in theatre with you – helping with the fetching and carrying, and putting up of all that blood. They've let me sit down for a while – but only if I let them 'bleed' me to give you some of my 'nurse' blood … I've donated many, many times over the years – but you've been the first patient I've been privileged to see actually receiving my blood – its trickling through as I write this!! Unlike the Estonians platelets, my blood has benefited from the occasional glass of red wine to give it quality (I have expensive taste in wine). Will come to see you in the morning. Maggie.

22.00: Mark, I'm off to my tent now, should have gone 2 hours ago, but couldn't leave until I knew you were OK. I've just counted up your blood usage: 45 blood, 36 plasma. Your co offered to bring some of the lads in to give you theirs! See you tomorrow. Karen X

09/05/09, 20.00–10/05/09, 8.00: Hi Mark, my name is Jill and I have been your nurse overnight. You have kept me busy Mark but I don't mind, we all want you to do well. Quite an eventful night, very unstable with your blood pressure, we needed to find two more units of blood and two FFP [fresh frozen plasma] for you. Dr Mathews has stayed up and spent most of the night at your bedside as have I. It makes me sad to see you so sick and I hope against hope that your condition improves. If your family get to read this my heart goes out to them. You have a brave son. Good luck. Jill.

I was operating at many automatic levels. I rang David and suggested that he come as soon as he could. I spoke to a neurologist friend about brain death and what it meant: could Mark recover if we left the machines on, what chance was there that he would wake again? He said that the brain stem stopping functioning was regarded as an alternative form of death to heart death: if one goes on ventilating in this situation the heart always stops eventually anyhow. So if there was no response to brain stem function tests there was no point in continuing ventilating. I was sleeping little, losing weight, eating without wanting to in echoing NHS lunch bars with washed tiled floors. There was no talk of the obvious and the deep, just the numbed surreal pain, all unsaid. From now my memory would let me down, sometimes unable to retain even simple straightforward things, leaving great gaps. It was as if I was in a strange slow nightmare and soon would wake. For a long time after this Mark would come home and all would be OK.

Mark's father arrived later that Monday. I was anxious about seeing him: we had not met for several years. We embraced when we met, courteous and clipped, but were unable to support one another.

I was surrounded by people. Several of Mark's friends came to Birmingham from London, and even one from Hong Kong who left as soon as he heard of Mark's injury, telling work and his girlfriend as he booked a flight in the taxi. Two families came, both close to Mark. They were all kept in another room somewhere but spent some precious time with us. Colonel Tom Bonas from the Welsh Guards visited for a day – he had been on a regimental battlefield tour with Mark to visit the war graves at the Somme, and so for him this awful tense time had more meaning. Two friends from London came one day each to be with us, cancelling their respective GP surgeries to do so, one leaving her son to take his first GCSE. We took it in turns to file in and have time with Mark.

It is hard to describe the upset of Mark's friends who managed to visit him at his bedside, talking to him and playing his 'awful' music to him to get him to stir before we switched off the machines. They were young people, audacious and full of dreams, struggling to understand not only the loss of their friend, their mate, saying goodbye to him for ever, but also that to live means to die.

Three close friends from school wrote in the hospital diary that had come from Bastion:

S: Alright mate. This reminds me of diary writing on our walk across Spain. You remember the start of the 'longest day'? 56 km on tarmac in 42 deg heat. We set off from that small odd hostel at about 5. It was early anyway. We both had pretty bad tendonitis and spent 20 mins getting our trainers on. You had that bloody ski pole like an American tourist to help your swollen knee. There was a small moment of doubt after about 3 hrs and 2 km about how sane we were to do this, but we pushed on through. I remember writing that after a day like that there was nothing that two stubborn friends could not achieve. We did alright you and I, eh? That rule of achievement was a maxim you followed your whole life. You excelled, and achieved, and led from the front. Life will never be the same without you, matey. There were so many more trips for you and me to do. Suppose I will just fly solo with you as my motivation.

So long mate so long.

I: Hi mate, I'm privileged to be able to write one last indecipherable note to you. I think I've known you longer than anyone else apart from my parents, and every minute has been a joy. So I'm lucky that it was you being a mate since the age of 5. I'm not sure who I'll play football in the park with, drink too many drinks with, traipse around Morocco with, but it won't be the same and I'll be thinking about you when I do. Too many happy memories – and there will always be a story about you to enliven every gathering. So you'll still be here. See you next time mate.

M: 'Markie mate' will be a catchphrase that will stay with me forever. I am trying to think of the best bits to write here but even those would fill a novel, from the day we met trying to convince you that despite the lack of rugby and height, Robinites was the right place. We all had a ball when you came along. All our PS periods together trying to convince Charlotte that working was so last season and our constant banter, usually around your latest near conquest deposited in the holly bush. Despite nearly losing you to the Aussie outback, it will forever be a privilege to have lived with you in Oxford, carrying on with little more maturity from where we had left off at school, running through the wall, making Jack Ass videos and the piece de resistance – you trying to leapfrog a mail box and spectacularly failing. We had some incredibly brilliant times out skiing – most of the time with you frightening the life out of mum with your idiotic big act on slalom skis, massive hangovers and teaching Toby every schoolboy trick in the book. Toby idolises you, something that I would never admit in person, but he will grow up with a big Mark influence and I imagine join the army just because you did. I cannot describe how much he loved you, demanding to be taken out of school if there was talk of you coming to Zeals. I could not have asked for a better friend and influence for him and me and I, along with my parents, will always cherish you for everything. I could go on for pages, the camper van trip, the road trips to Durham, the skiing, holidays, school, university, London, and I will be forever grateful that you dropped by, where in true Mark style you made an immediate impact on all who you met. We will miss you and never forget the fun and zest you brought to my life. All my love M.

I asked if I could talk to Guardsman Stuart Gizzie, who had come on the same aeroplane with Mark, injured with bullets through both ankles. At the time I knew very little about what had happened and wanted to know more. He agreed to speak on the Tuesday morning but must have worried about that. I knew that he might be shocked and even guilty that he had survived; my issues had to be put aside. He must have felt the same. I walked in and he said, 'I am sorry,' as we hugged one another, both tearful. He told me how Mark was 'one of the boys' but had been an admired leader and respected soldier as well. He never shouted, always smiled, and there was his wonderful sense of humour. He organised games for them in the evening in that dry hot dusty old fort, no mod cons, no life as they knew it, just fighting and all there together. Under velvet skies they played *The Army's Got Talent*, with Mark as Amanda Holden, and *Deal or No Deal*. I felt proud when he said that Mark had chosen to deal with minor infringements and transgressions in an admirably fair and non-humiliating way, by a fines book. All sat around in a circle and agreed a suitable fine, the total added to a pot to be used for a trip to Blackpool when they got back. Mark was once fined £15 for leaving his gun behind. He was their mate when they went downtown in Aldershot, 'the boss' when soldiering.

Gdsm Gizzie was still in the world where Mark was alive – it was just three days since they had fought together and, despite everything, he just wanted to go back to be with the boys, his brothers in arms. I could not ask how Mark had died; I did not have the heart to.

On that Tuesday David and I sat in clinical silence whilst the two consultants carried out brain stem tests, explaining what they were doing in flat perfunctory voices. It was calm and light in the room as they tried to get a reaction from him and his brain, any flicker of life. This was the first time I realised he was dead, the first time there was no hope. David did the second set of tests with them without me – I could not bear watching his still, unresponsive body.

We all said goodbye to Mark, privately, in and out of the room in turn. At about 11 a.m. we switched off the machines. I watched the spirit leave Mark in less than a second as his face changed and his lips tinged blue. We were bringing our son's life to an end. But there was no life there to be had, it had all gone.

It was over. We all went home. I would not have anticipated the rest.

CHAPTER 2

MOURNING AND BURIAL

Mourning is a kind of madness. It is a very long walk through dark subterranean parts of one's mind where reason and fact hardly exist. Maybe that hackneyed word 'losing' a loved one in its own way reflects it best. If you lose something you want to find it. In the early stages of grief this was how I was: I could go to where Mark was and perhaps find him. My own death became less terrifying than in the past, even welcoming. In the clear light of day, I was held back by knowing that for family and friends to lose another would be too much. But often I felt that it was impossible to live without ever seeing Mark again, it would be too long and too painful, I just could not do it.

I felt as if a large part of me had died; I had lost myself as I had lost Mark, the person I knew inside was no longer there. In this new private world I was unable to reach out, to care for those close to me. Elizabeth and I felt apart, not able to cross the void between us. I stopped seeing my partner John, guilty because I had nothing to give. My world was suddenly grey, lifeless, dead, and I felt numb. The dark hinterland felt very attractive and it would have been easy to slip into it, at peace and alone with my memories.

It was often better and easier to think that Mark was abroad, in America, and would come home soon. I knew so well that warm, understanding smile, that young love flowing without guile, that cocked head and lithe body, that gentle affectionate nagging, the smell of his hair on his pillow still so strong. Of course he was here, somewhere. At times I called him Markie and willed him to walk towards me along the pavement, around a corner, and his only response was that he could not, it was just too hard for him.

Sometimes I felt as if he had walked away, rejected me. I said to myself that as his life went on it was always going to be this way. Perhaps as he moved on, with a life mate and new demands, our closeness would have always waned, it was just now rather than then. I knew it would be hard at any time.

For many months there was a sense of wanting to go back to before this happened and the frustration of not being able to. Time would not turn around, however much I wanted it to. This wanting to live as I had, now so strong, was a very new feeling – not wanting to be here in the present but in the before. It must be the stuff of all those who mourn, who regret.

Mark's death swallowed up my life and thoughts of it would not let go of me. It was as if my love for him, reaching out, was suddenly stopped and had nowhere to go, searched for expression, unable to find it. I tried to talk about it but I could not find the words; I spoke about Mark instead, wanting him to be there. I filled the house with photographs, reminding me of the person who felt as if he was still there but could not be. The frustration of it. If the bell or telephone went late at night, my sleepy mind would breathe a sigh of relief: he was back, it was all a bad dream.

Early mornings were nearly always difficult. But at any time I could find myself in surprising situations suddenly moist-eyed and feeling out of control, a hot painful lava under the calm skin of my daily composure suddenly erupting through a crack. The Army returned a parcel I had sent Mark before he died, which he had not received. In it was the packet of Bird's custard, one of his childhood loves, and my letter chatting about the happy minutiae of daily life in the time before he had died. That was where I wanted to be, and I cried and cried.

Occasionally I would be reminded of the unfairness of it. No one from Southwark, a huge sprawling inner-city borough, had died at war for many years, nor from his schools, nor from the Welsh Guards, and his was now only the second death in the battalion of 400 soldiers. Why Mark? Was it because he was inexperienced and new? Had I made a mistake, been too relaxed about it? Should I have done something else? I knew that he had chosen this way – he was doing what he wanted to do and loved doing – but should I have tried harder to make him more aware of its dangers, see death another way? When he left I asked him, almost pleaded with him, not to take any risks, to look after himself, but was that enough? This guilt would often come back, creeping, irrational.

Slowly, as I wandered the paths of mourning, I found myself thinking other things. I thought maybe it was better that way: Mark was one of the 'lads that will die in his glory and never be old', as A. E. Housman had put it in *A Shropshire Lad*. Perhaps it was meant to be, there was a purpose, the world might be richer and not poorer for his death. He died because if he had not, others fighting with him would have done so instead. He may have left a legacy: not to be forgotten in his death as he may have been in life. Others said he would be at peace.

I am not a believing Christian, but the pain was so powerful that I needed to know if Mark was somewhere, and so I struggled with spiritual belief. I knew that many before me had turned to the refuge and the comfort of it. Mark's soldiers did the same, young men trying to reconcile their memories of him and of that awful time, the smell of his blood over their shoulders. Now he might be in a better place. He might be here, around. But I was not even ready to have him join a heavenly throng, other spirits – it felt too anonymous when his voice and smells were still here.

Yet if one said it was just the end, no more, then that did not make sense to me either. The spirits of this world surely live on, in memories, in dreams, in what they have done and how they have been. They leave those wordless traces – it is them.

And so Mark's death brought me closer to religion. I felt its purpose: to help those left behind who feel they have no answers and that this is too big for them. Its rituals were ways to bring one closer to the calm that allows one to accept, to feel the wide canvas and the understanding of many ages. I could see the anguish of others close to me, their struggle with his death; in the end they had to reach their own peace in their own way. And I could see that religion pointed a path, a very well-worn path.

After Mark's death people wrote letters in their hundreds to comfort me and the family, perhaps to comfort themselves. I have reread them many times. They came from all quarters: complete strangers, neighbours, work colleagues, Army comrades, friends. There were letters from senior Army officers and generals; even the Prime Minister, who apparently wrote to the families of all soldiers killed in action, and Prince Charles, looking after those in his regiments. Some were particularly touching. Brigadier Tim Radford, heading the 19th Brigade in Afghanistan at the time, wrote:

> … he was charming, utterly focused, thoughtful and he left an indelible stamp. I know that his soldiers adored him and that he was held in such high esteem by them.

One of his friends told me on the day of the incident that Mark was described by his soldiers as having 'a face that was sculpted by angels'. In twenty-five years in the Army I have never heard soldiers speak with such affection about one of their officers ...

The days before the funeral felt tense, dry, unreal, like death. Such events nudge relationships. I was very touched that my younger sister and her daughter, my niece, stopped their lives in Australia to come immediately to help. They stayed and became all-important, understanding quickly the nuances of my social life and my friends in London, politely and calmly dealing with the constant telephone calls and visits, setting up a perfumery of beautiful flowers. My brother arrived just before the funeral and remained with me after, also a great comfort. My sister-in-law arrived from the Bahamas with her daughter, always friends despite the divorce.

I came to realise that this dark, sad, inexplicable side of life was understood by so many. People struggled with words; they were simply too difficult, just cheap messengers for feelings. Instead they gave us casseroles, huge cakes, and flowers, other things which would do what words could not do and make this less of a lonely place.

Soon after Mark's death, David left for the solace of his sculpture studio and friends in Berlin, agreeing that he would contribute to the funeral plans from there. This situation irritated our past animosities as we both struggled with our particular reactions to Mark's death. But despite all this, we had to make decisions, hard and new decisions, at this tragic time. Before he left, we looked at the overgrown, crowded and immense graveyards of south London. They were nearby but they felt so wrong – these were old graves, usually old people. We decided Mark's body would be cremated and his ashes buried in a military cemetery. It felt an important and difficult decision.

The Welsh Guards offered a military funeral in the Guards Chapel at the Wellington Barracks, St James's Park, and then were quietly comforting and supportive in its arrangement, suggesting options, practising it beforehand. At the time this was the first officer the Welsh Guards had lost in battle for many years, and it felt as if it was a shock to them also. As more soldiers and officers died in the following months they tried so hard to do their best by them, very sensitive to the wishes of the families of their dead. I was touched that they arranged for Gdsm Gizzie to come all the way from Birmingham to the funeral, in his wheelchair or on crutches, mourning Mark; the rest of the platoon was still in Afghanistan.

Mark's funeral was held in late May. A police escort of fourteen motorcycles led the hearse with its flag-draped coffin and the entourage, stopping all the traffic from my home. Past the hospital where he had been born, through the patches of struggling poverty in Southwark, across

huge busy intersections now still, past the stone magnifi-
cence of those anonymous institutions lining the Thames,
Big Ben and the Houses of Parliament, and finally to
the chapel in Birdcage Walk. We sat silent in our wide-
windowed cars, Elizabeth, my brother and me. It was
a muted and yet intense experience, the strangeness of
one's inside self coinciding with the silence of those well-
known streets as the police escort quietened all in front.
People walking on their way paused and watched, quiet
and still, or doffed their hats or crossed themselves.

Over 900 people came to the funeral: soldiers, officers
in braided uniforms, young beautiful girls, friends and
family, all together mourning Mark's going, their tears
sometimes more painful because of their own deep fears
for their partners and loved ones, or memories of lost
mates. That airy cube of a building with its beautiful original portico and altar became a place of grandeur for ninety
minutes. It is lined with battered regimental flags which
hang aloft along the walls; Mark's coffin draped with the
Union flag was the centre of it all. Inexpressibly beautiful music was everywhere. That music took the place of
so many unspoken words, and hymns written to lift and
comfort did so, allowing that old and odd power, singing, to get us to a place of peace. The band played Elgar's
'Nimrod', and Mark's former cello teacher played Fauré's
haunting 'Après Un Rêve', which so powerfully echoed
the grief of all and said everything without one word.
Bach's 'Cello Suite No. 1' seemed to describe life going

on endlessly despite its highs and lows. David Butt Philip sang 'A Shropshire Lad' beautifully and slowly, its music composed by George Butterworth before his own death in the trenches of the First World War at the age of thirty-one. Poetry and wise words tried to explain, to make sense, to comfort. Elizabeth and Sholto, Mark's close friend from school, were both only in their twenties, but they spoke very movingly and with huge courage and understanding to all those people. Colonel Sandy Malcolm talked about Mark and the Army, and how he was sure that Mark's actions that day had saved lives. I also spoke, as I wanted that ethereal, formal and incredibly beautiful service to be about Mark as a person, as we all knew him. I said then that he would always be on my shoulder and in my heart. It was a wonderful farewell, and it felt important for those who wanted Mark to have something when he had just lost everything. But for most it was a chance to cry.

After the funeral the same police escort took us through Wellington Arch to the crematorium in west London. I was surprised that we went through the arch, but I realised that this was the Army burying their dead, a tribute to a Guards officer lost in battle. When we drove up to the chapel the police escort lined the path, heads bowed down to arms folded stiff with respect on their motorcycles, a simple formal gesture yet somehow profound. Mark's father spoke at this short powerful service, before the curtains were drawn and the casket with Mark's body was gone. As it went, outside a bugler played the 'Last Post' and rifles fired loud punctuating shots in a final military salute.

It was several months before I could watch a tape of the funeral and appreciate its beauty and what it meant to all – I felt hardly there. This was the death of my boy; why this public formality and ritual? It has taken me a long time to understand that it has its roots in the heroism of war death, words which mean so little and so much, tied up as they are with the ideals and anguish of centuries past. The 'ultimate sacrifice' is the reason for all the pomp and circumstance that followed Mark's death, the public respect for a private commitment. But at the time that aspect of Mark's death seemed almost impossible for me to comprehend – all I could think was that I had lost my child. People said I must be proud, but that had no meaning to me. Proud to lose my boy? Why?

Many weeks later we buried Mark's ashes at Brookwood Military Cemetery, Surrey. His grave joined a tidy line of small white tablets, each stone a symbol of a life lived and lost. When I first left him here I felt as if I were abandoning him to a cold and unknown world of spirits. The pines whispered nearby, haunted in the evenings and half-light. It felt impossibly desolate and lonely – for both of us, Mark and me – and I left him there very unwillingly. This sense of Mark as a spirit at one with the elements, the wind and the light, felt surreal, unsettling and incomprehensible. Surely that tangible person in the photograph by my bed, that person I could almost but not quite touch, was not of that world.

Slowly, over several months, Brookwood became a place of great comfort, of peace. Landscaped after the First World War with that particular congruent tension of formality and sprawling delight, its green mottled lawns are broken up by the rows of gravestones, gentle breezes stir patches of wild grass, and tall pines are uncompromising in their elegance. As I sat there, I often thought about the meaning of all this.

These beautiful landscaped vistas are a tribute for ever to all those soldiers who in the end have done what we could not, given up their precious young lives for someone else, something else. It was most likely to be their mates, in battle, when they matter more than oneself. I have tried to understand this, and I asked young men who still want to go or return to Afghanistan: does it not matter that you might die? They think not. I have heard them say that to die for one's country is an honourable death, that there are 'worse ways to go', and that dying is a risk they are prepared to take. Perhaps they are too naïve to be frightened of it, to understand why it is important to keep living and what life may bring; too young to have had time to know what it is to die because they have not had time to live. When Mark died, did he understand? He was doing what he had to do, but he must have known at that moment what he was giving up here, the life he had loved. In that moment of truth, if he felt regret it was too late.

There is an area at Brookwood reserved for those fallen in Afghanistan, and there is often a new grave when I visit – a young man whom Mark might have known and who would have heard about him. Perhaps they are still looking after one another. Bryan Smith, a gardener at the cemetery, tells the stories of those buried there. I chatted to him once whilst visiting and he instantly knew Mark, calling him by his first name as if he were an old friend. I found it odd at the time that strangers cared.

This was a strange new world but somehow shared. Other mothers and wives also lost their sons and husbands, and I was introduced to some of them. We remained close for years after, surprised by how similar we were in how we felt, how our grief felt as we struggled with our disbelief. That was a comfort to me, a marker of some strange normality. Over two years later, another mother said to me that with the death of her son she had lost the self that she knew. I understood that. The love of a child is a particular love. Our children are connected to us endlessly by a metaphorical umbilical cord. When they die, part of ourselves dies. Afterwards that protecting, giving, loving part of me tied up with Mark for many years was gone for ever.

Two Army officers, both veterans of several tours, told me later how they understood for the first time the impact of a young death on wives, mothers, families.

One was changed by the birth of his own son; the other, himself the father of two small children, had given news of the death of a soldier son to the young man's mother, and finally decided to leave the Army.

It felt to me as if an early death is almost kept a silent secret, rather like the trauma of birth, part of human experience for centuries but too painful for others to know. Friends told me of mothers and sisters changed for ever by deaths in earlier wars. Or perhaps early death is by now almost forgotten as times change: this is a generation with less experience of death, and often no religion to turn to for explanation and hope. Was it different for these young men now?

A number of services were held in the months after the funeral as many struggled with Mark's death. His old school, Charterhouse, held a service on Memorial Sunday. It is a school with a past rich with a sense of duty, and boys like Mark who lost their lives in the two world wars. The boys there now, spotty and humbled by what this meant, sang as I have rarely heard singing, alive with respect and admiration: one of them had dared to die in a hot dusty wasteland in a wild country.

The Welsh Guards returned from their six-month tour in October. We had a regimental service in the wooden garrison church in Aldershot in early December, the men restless and silent in uniform. Seven candles were slowly carried down the aisle for each of their seven dead and put on the altar. This was military mourning for an aching private pain. Many of the soldiers had been with Mark and were still dealing with their own memories and grief. Those Welsh soldiers had obeyed Mark, admired him, laughed with him and fought beside him, they had brought him back and were with him when he spoke his last words. Like me, they found it easy to blame themselves afterwards, imagining how it might have been different so that he could still be with them.

After the service the soldiers marched proudly through the streets of Aldershot, the locals clapping. Perhaps some who had grieved understood.

There were other occasions of public mourning that I was invited to, I think to help me with my sadness, to help me understand that I was not alone and that others were suffering also. In early 2010 we all sang together at the 19th Brigade service at St Anne's Cathedral in Belfast for the eighty soldiers who had died in the past year. The sermon suggested optimistically that whilst Belfast had once been a place of war, today it was peaceful. Perhaps now I could see the point of that struggle, those lost lives. But the cost of conflict was there at the reception as all were quiet with their private grief.

In June 2010 we were invited to a family memorial service in the National Arboretum, which I found hard to bear even then, a year after Mark's death. We were seated in the inner circle of high white stone walls, the names of this year's dead recently engraved on them. The brightness of the day and the hot walls underlined for me the horror of that hot thirsty death and men desperate for help. Nearby was a large sculpture in tortured dark metal of a limp soldier being carried on a stretcher by his men. I sat there, tight, hard inside, trying not to cry, not to feel.

It would be nice to say there were good times as well. Certainly I went to parties, laughing and enjoying the distraction. People were very kind and I got on with my life, forced to do so by work commitments and by well-meaning friends who would ask me out if I wavered. But underneath was that thick black blanket, that seemingly endless weed in the summer pond: my early morning fantasies about Mark's death were violent and bloody, destroying all light and any hope. Someone at a party said it would take a long time to get over, and at the time that comment felt impossible, a life sentence. I left the party.

I knew that I had to choose words to put on Mark's headstone, but it was months before I could find them and his grave was left unmarked. These few words had to *be* Mark, and to stand for him with family and friends for many years. Finally they were chosen, and at 11 a.m. on 28 January 2011 the Army padre blessed Mark's new head-stone, surrounded by young officer friends, Elizabeth and me. Prayers finished at about 11.10 and, as they ended, a shaft of light found its way through the thick grey winter cloud, lighting up this headstone for ten minutes. It was ethereal with light, the only one of the thousands there.

Hardly an hour went by without thinking of Mark. Slowly the immediate disbelief and struggle with the reality of his death went. Much later, I realised 'accepting Mark's death' meant knowing in my heart and not only my head that he had died. That time was in many ways the hardest, when I was just beginning to understand. It took a long time, well over two years, before the first glimmer of real awareness and certainty came, and one morning I looked at his photograph and knew that he had gone.

I now understood the beautiful words of war poet Siegfried Sassoon, read at Mark's funeral:

Everyone suddenly burst out singing:
And I was fill'd with such delight
As prison'd birds must find in freedom
Winging wildly across the white
Orchards and dark-green fields; on; on; and out of sight.

Everyone's voice was suddenly lifted,
And beauty came with the setting sun.
My heart was shaken with tears; and horror
Drifted away ... O but everyone
Was a bird; and the song was wordless; and the singing
will never be done.

My heart had been shaken by tears, my horror finally drifted away. But I was still of this world.

CHAPTER 3

MARK

The long factual road of Mark's history, the valedictory letters and words that others have used all feel a pale account of him, warm with life. With time, holes should fill. But there can never be anyone to take Mark's place, that one star has gone. That great gap has now only memories of happy times to paper over it. Mark did his bit in his short life, giving others things to hang onto and dwell on for a long time, the stuff of the rest of all our lives – those memories, what he taught us, the sad sweet Mark smell of his clothes in his drawer, and the collected oddments that mean him.

Each person whose life brushed up against Mark's was left with their own store to dip into, to savour, to reminisce about. Friends and family had deeper wells, and the endless work of remembering was muddied by the heavy sadness of loss.

Mark seemed almost a hero before he died. As a child he was blond, sweet-faced, naughty and endearing. As an adult he was handsome, and his soldiers dubbed him '007. He had a body that moved well – boyish, slim, fit and robust, a Michelangelo's David with an elegant Roman face. He was very charming but unaware of it, and I knew few who could be so witty; unknown Irish forebears had taught him how to weave a tale as others fell about laughing. He was intelligent and bright but not academic, wise for his age with the ways of the world and with an immediate understanding of people and situations. There was his feeling for music and sensitivity to things aesthetic. Not least was his idealism, perhaps influenced by his grandfathers, both men of unusual vision in their own ways. Then there was his energy and hope, his natural optimism, his relaxed manner, his warmth and his thoughtfulness. Those whom he met, however junior or senior, were treated respectfully as equals. On one occasion, just before he left, we were enjoying the celebratory ritual of tea and cake on the terrace at home, all fun and talk, and yet he went off quietly to give the gardener some of the cake. He always loved being at home, its ordinariness, and seemed almost to revel in it. He cared about others, and everyone loved him.

At the funeral, Sholto described his schoolboy memories:

Mark was a different sort of person from most of us.

Yes, he had any number of rare and admirable traits, which have filled the tributes, press releases and recollections in the last couple of weeks.

But he also lacked a couple of things which made him

even rarer. He lacked inhibition and he lacked prejudice. And it was because of this, in addition to his enthusiasm, charm, motivation, courage and countless more besides, that has led to this chapel being filled with such an eclectic mix of people today. Wherever he went, and whoever he met, he was very much on home turf.

I think it would take decades to meet all of Mark's friends, and would take you to places that you would not dream of, but somehow Mark managed to fit us all in, in the length of his tragically short life.

Throughout, Mark was never one to hang around or turn down a challenge. Whether he was excelling at the cello, planning record – and unfortunately bank – breaking trips to the South Pole, salvaging sheep from nests of brown snakes in the Outback, or leading his men from the front in Afghanistan, Mark made sure that he was in the thick of it.

Those things that most of us would find difficult, or would be apprehensive about, Mark seemed to approach with optimism and confidence. And while this may not always have had firm grounding in precise and experienced knowledge, he still managed to pull the thing off in the end. His tenacity and determination went hand-in-hand with his enthusiasm and motivation, and he was perfectly reflected, both in personality and physique, by Nutmeg his Jack Russell.

And he was fearless.

Mark would rarely dwell on the downside of anything.

He never saw the seemingly obvious dangers of making nettle soup or the disastrous consequences of attempting a back-flip on skis before mastering the snow-plough turn. Instead he would turn his attention to why he was doing something, and how much fun and adventure he could squeeze out of it.

I distinctly remember questioning Mark whether he really thought it was good idea to hurtle down a steep hill on a home-made skateboard into a barbed wire fence … with no brakes. He shrugged and put it down to being a case of 'simple physics'. He would just jump off before he got to the fence. Of course he would …

He was as infuriating as he was boundlessly enjoyable to be around. He froze his housemates' trainers into huge blocks of ice, relocated sleeping guests' cars at more than one twenty-first birthday party, set fire to his friends' hair and shaved off their eyebrows. And yet, despite this, every one of those involved, included or damaged by Mark is here today.

The concepts of 'giving up' or of 'just leaving it' did not tend to register with Mark. We can all remember numerous times when we would find ourselves deeper into something than we would be comfortable with. Invariably, before you could bear a grudge, his grinning face would join you in the freezing Welsh pool, followed by his unnervingly naked body, and he would always be the first to make the round of tea afterwards.

I would like, on behalf of all his friends, to pay tribute

to one of the bravest, most charming, most enthusiastic, most joyful, most loving, smallest – and yet largest – men ever to walk, run, ride, cycle, canoe, ski, motorbike, drive, swim, and even sledge the earth.

Let us not forget how Mark has touched us all, and how all those things that made him who he was have rubbed off on each and every one of us. Perhaps, after all, the greatest things in a man are those that are left behind.

This was Mark as he was to the world he knew.

For me as his mother, those memories went back much further, to those anxious times of babyhood and childhood. Mark's beginnings were tenuous and represented, in many ways, 'low odds' from the start. I remember the night of his conception, a sleepy cuddle in the middle of the night and suddenly I was pregnant, unplanned, despite contraception. We had only recently arrived in Berlin for a stay of six months, then a cultured and bohemian city scarred by war and its living detritus, the Berlin Wall. It was a time of exciting local museum visits and trips to the east side of the city, and walks in very deep snow. One memory stands out: my baby girl's first birthday cake. It had one candle and was baked by a local *hausfrau* with that old Berlin hospitality, only days after we arrived.

Almost nine months later, on 17 July 1982, I was having a usual Saturday breakfast back in London. Less than an hour after that, Mark was born on the floor of a corridor in a local hospital, no time for help with my pain but perhaps less birth trauma for him. This was Mark, forever eager to be there, black-haired, beautiful, healthy, 8 lb 6 oz. Elizabeth, speaking well by then at twenty months, was cautious about this new thing.

Weeks later he smiled, very early. But over the coming months he became a sickly child, and this regular struggle with his chronic health issues probably made us closer, the lioness in me protecting her cub. He was difficult to feed: he seemed to have no appetite and would often turn his face away. I was confused, unsure what to do, and soon the GP noticed. I was told after registering at the hospital that it might be my breast milk that disagreed with him, the reason why his weight was seriously trailing. Now I had two small children, both waking at night, including one who was very thin and whose system was not working well. When Mark was ill he was usually very ill, and he had baby pneumonia more than once. As a visiting doctor said to me, one needed a stethoscope to find out how his lungs were, his smile was a traitor. Doctors tried to help but often did not have the correct answers. In the end, age sorted out his body. But his life for about five years would be shaped by those early experiences of illness and deafness. His response seemed to be to ignore it.

Perhaps that early illness was what made him so determined, the person who as an adult on a university ski trip kept trying to successfully perfect a very challenging ski jump and 360-degree turn long after all others had fallen and given up. A video taken at the time shows his presence of mind as he finally skied gracefully down the slope, took off and slowly turned in the air completely, to land safely and ski ahead. As a very young child he seemed quite oblivious to danger, and when I told him not to run into the street, the cars might knock him down, his eyes lit up with the curiosity of what might happen. As he grew older that early fearlessness and his determination had taught him lessons, and later knitted into an acute strategic awareness and a strong sense of what would work effectively and what would not.

His black baby hair blew away in the wind one day in Wales and he became what he always was, a laughing blond little boy, an irrepressible spirit, curious to the extreme as he tried to find out about this world. He crawled by five months, walked by nine. He was usually uninterested in obedience, as his hazel eyes lit up with the pleasure of the unknown, the almost impossible. I knew that this child would have to be shaped by praise rather than punishment, otherwise his small life would be all trouble. I used simple rules – 'no being rude to adults' and 'no hurting other children' – and then tried to ignore the rest as much as I could, leaving age, life and other influences to mould him. His naughtiness was frustrating and tiring, and I can remember feeling guilty as I took a trip abroad alone to see my unwell father, relieved to be without him. But I was usually always there, and trust became part of his life and later of him, the reason others took to him. People always trusted him.

He was not allowed playmates at home or to go to nursery school until almost four years old because of the risk of infection, so Elizabeth was his friend, and they would bring their lively play and games to our quiet life at home, busying themselves with each other. His sister was a still, gentle soul – she was the one in the middle of the playground who watched the other children, and he was the one who was gone in a minute. Later, as Elizabeth discovered books and they became her friends, he railed that he had no one to play with; he wanted a younger brother or sister.

Slowly Mark's playground became the leafy suburbs of south London. He played football in the local park and began to make 'friends' – not real friends then but co-explorers, each adventure an effort to prise open a new world. Later they became real friends, trusting one another from then and pushing on together, safe with their memories of those days.

He continued to be naughty and to test boundaries, but always with that endearing smile. At about seven years old he went to Cadbury Bourneville with friends, where they had a morning of free chocolate tasting. He was the only one of several children who turned pale as we left the building and was sick in the park.

There is a great deal of happiness from this time.

There were occasional holidays in France, a gastro-nomic and cultural mystery. But mostly it was Cornwall and lonely beaches, windswept cliffs, teas with thick yellow cream and sweet red jam, battered fish eaten surrounded by damp boats and gulls eagle-eyed for crumbs. The joy of clear cold water and young wriggling bodies. To be back in the sea when they were at home again, they (over)filled the bath with cold water, so that the bathwater dripped through the ceiling of the hall below.

We had little money since I had stopped work, partly because of Mark's illness. David was working as a sculptor and was often abroad teaching. I was at home as Mark's childhood very slowly unfolded, and I saw it through these new eyes, brimming with hope, always reminding me of the magic of it.

We went to New York for four months in 1986, when Mark was four, David working at an art school in Brooklyn. There Mark wrote a first diary, drawing a picture of the Twin Towers. We rented a book-lined house locally and could often hear the crack of gunfire through the hot night. We occasionally went into 'dangerous' non-white suburbs outside Brooklyn to explore small local muse-ums, days spent with black skins all around and the sense of being tense and alone in an unknown area. A truck driver shouted abuse at us for Mark and his white pretti-ness, and I understood concretely then how your skin can set you apart, define you for others.

There were markers, some school-driven. Mark was young for his year and he would sometimes be sick with anxiety when going to school because he could not read. There had been a proverbial burning of the old books at the local primary, and Mark did not take to the phonetic reading scheme that they introduced. He needed routine and old ways of teaching, so we decided he was to go to the nearby preparatory school, only affordable if we moved house and so lost our mortgage.

Two years later, perhaps because the headmaster sensed some talent despite him being a poor reader, Mark was accepted into Dulwich College Preparatory School; the proviso was that he was tutored beforehand and had remedial teaching once at the school. I welcomed the suggestion: I had been impressed by *My Early Career* by Winston Churchill, also a late starter, who attributed his subsequent love of language to that early remedial experience with its more individual teaching. Mark also grew to love language and reading. Those difficulties during his junior preparatory schools seemed to give Mark an understanding of the 'other side', and he was always kind to those struggling.

Many hours were spent together sitting on the sofa at that time, me helping Mark with the things he found difficult – his reading as he lost interest when he realised he could not get to the end of a book, and times tables, which were difficult to absorb because of some dyslexia and so needed hundreds of repetitions. We read books together about other lives, such as the story of a boy in a monastery in the fifteenth century, and adventure stories, Scott of the Antarctic and many others. We lived these together and were both fascinated. Until he died, Mark continued to read and collect books about young explorers and their stories of endurance, heroism and pain.

Mark's first teacher at DCPS, Miss Maynard, wrote after his death:

> I still have the most vivid memories of when Mark was in my class aged seven. He was always such a sunny little boy, courteous and well behaved, energetic and a real tryer. I too remember that ever-present smile. He was always responsive and keen to learn ... I was fortunate enough to meet him again last year. I was so thrilled and flattered that (a) he remembered me and (b) that he wanted to return to his old classroom and find me. There I was with yet another group of wonderful little lads setting up the art task we were about to launch into. 'Miss Maynard, there are some visitors outside who want to come in!' said my boys. Well, we get visitors regularly, so I brushed aside their words and assured them the visitors would come in when they were ready. And they did. I shall treasure those minutes with Mark. What a charming young man! He was so at ease and lovely with the boys. They, of course, adored meeting a real soldier. Yesterday (the funeral) was the most marvellous celebration of Mark and his life ... I left with pockets full of

soggy tissues but a sense that the gap between Mark aged seven in 1M and the charming young man I met last year had been filled for me. What a life. What a lover of life. How full those years had been. What an incredibly special young man Mark had grown up to be.

George Marsh, the headmaster for most of Mark's time, remembered:

[Mark] was so enthusiastic to be part of the heartbeat of the Prep. He did everything to the best of his ability. He was small but he played sport against boys much bigger than himself. He was a terrier on the rugby field. He was very fit and I seem to remember him scoring tries late in games or when I thought the move had died … he was never short of a word and never short of friends to talk to or play with. He liked being part of a group. He was both a leader and did not mind being led.

Although initially 'remedial', to my surprise Mark was the one pushed up into the next stream at the end of each year. The school offered much for him. His eyes lit up at the delights of nature study, staking our own square metre of mud and undergrowth in the local woods and carefully recording temperature, rain and the movement of tiny animals over two weeks. He did a project on Constable and Turner, and together we looked at their great works in art galleries, surprised by the unexpected synergies of the two artists. There was rugby and all the formal outlets for his endless energy, his running, free golf coaching; I had to limit his exercise to give him time to read, to think, to eat. His creative self grasped at the opportunities offered at the school, and he was finally given the acting prize for his part in the school play, *Home from Home*, based on the school evacuation to Wales during the war. He must have thought about war then.

It was about now that he taught himself the piano, listening in the corner to his sister's lessons. He began to learn the cello and the piano. If he could not play he could sing, and both became important to him.

Alastair Blayden, sub-principal cellist with the London Symphony Orchestra, became Mark's cello teacher early in his teens. Alastair, perhaps twenty years his senior but like Mark with an intense love of music, became an important figure to him. Mark had perfect pitch, and though he hated practising he would want to listen to the end of a piece of music on the radio even if late for something else. Alastair always said he could take his music further but Mark did not want to be a musician. Nevertheless, his cello became as important to him as his rugby.

Mark moved to Dulwich College at eleven, after my interview with the headmaster across a huge leather desk. This was now big school. The school offered him his beloved rugby, wonderful music and a wider world, all within walking distance of home. He loved the Combined Cadet Force, it naturally followed on from many cub and scout camps as a boy. He continued to shine at all sports, a natural athlete. He played scrum half in the college second rugby team, sometimes injured in those Saturday games. He learned about pain, as he lay in the local hospital A&E concussed or with a leg injury, once next to an old man moaning and crying out in anguish.

Although streamed in the top set of classes at Dulwich College, Mark then had years of erratic academic achievement – flashes of solid performance then lack of interest, always underpinned by detentions and the slightly glazed and tired faces of his secondary school teachers when I met them. I was very pleased when he sat the same GCSE examination on the same day as Elizabeth. Aged sixteen she achieved an A-star whilst Mark, then just fourteen, gained an A. But taming Mark academically was always a challenge and enlightened teachers helped. Famously he told an A-level teacher to 'chill out'.

Mark's father left the family to live abroad and make art in Berlin when Mark was eleven, and we separated. David would see the children on his short trips to the UK every one or two months; I became a single mother, working part-time and with very little money. We were a close-knit little threesome. Elizabeth was always very important to Mark; she was more studious but kind, and they balanced one another out. Except for childish arguments and pranks, and the usual short teen-age stages when they professed not to like one another, they remained very close friends through to adult life.

We had bought a new house in terrible condition at the time of the separation, and very slowly renovated it. The kitchen was the hub of family life, the scene of many raucous family meals and attempts at discipline, during which Elizabeth and Mark would join forces to support the other as I tried to negotiate with two recalcitrant teenagers across the kitchen table. It was where we loved to be despite its ancient stained linoleum, its old furniture and the gas oven on four legs with no heat thermostat and a bent door in which we regularly cooked ambitious cakes and dinners.

With my encouragement the two would sail small dinghies with children from local Southwark estates at the Surrey Quays Sailing Club, free sailing for those who had little to do in their summer holidays. They would come home surprised and sometimes shocked by the angry behaviour of some of the teenagers, but I encouraged them to try to see the person behind. As a single mother I was sometimes considered socially disadvantaged, although living in a wealthy middle class area. I wanted both of them to understand this.

We continued to holiday in Cornwall and had a regular rented cottage at Porthleven. We would all drive down with the dog, windows open, loud music, listening to a favourite and very beautiful recording of Jacqueline

Du Pré playing the cello. Mark, of course, would be the one to dive off the cliffs into the deep rock pools below, and wanted to be out with the local lads late at night on the beach whilst I fretted at home.

They were generous, loving children. As teenagers they took me to Florence for my birthday, paying for very cheap fares on a 4 a.m. flight and even cheaper noisy accommodation. We had such fun, visiting wonderful galleries, climbing steep and exhausting towers and monuments together, eating Italian ice-cream and cakes. Later we would often go away as a family for my birthday celebrations, once a frozen cottage in a Welsh valley in January and then a surprise party back home in London that they organised for me.

Mark became part of other families' holidays, too – skiing, golfing and at the seaside. He developed a love of the countryside and country life, and of Scotland, fishing and hunting there later.

Both children reached their peak of outrageous behaviour at fourteen. Mark was to go to an overnight party at a local friend's, and all the boys invited secretly planned to take alcohol there. Mark was cat-feeding for a friend of mine in their large house with a wine cellar and he stole one or two bottles of wine. Of course, they were caught, and tears were metaphorically shed. I insisted that he go to my friends, a tall imposing couple, and admit and apologise. He found that difficult, scrawny and underconfident as he was, but although so ashamed he was able to do it. A lesson well learned, as he later understood the need to apologise for his transgressions.

David and I had always taken Mark and Elizabeth to art galleries when young, to the point when they would refuse to go, unable to see the art, more interested in play. Mark continued to go to galleries – some with his father in Berlin; later with me in Paris or Florence. We would close our minds to names and descriptions, trying to use our eyes alone to see and understand. He had a good eye and revelled in it. He could see why a painting or a building was beautiful, why it worked, why it was all wrong. He had an innate sensibility and understanding of all things aesthetic.

After a two-week free trial of boarding at Dulwich College, Mark decided he wanted to leave home to go to boarding school, to be without an elder sister and a mother forever cajoling and funnelling his energies into sensible activities. I was keen that he had other influences on him than us, more close male influences, a firm housemaster who could demand more than I could. I said that he would have to win a scholarship for funding and I encouraged him to apply. So he played one of Bach's six Cello Suites very slowly to win a music scholarship to Charterhouse School in Surrey for his A-levels.

Rather surprisingly to me, he did well in his GCSEs, and so he left home for the first time as a young sixth former, playing his piano and cello and singing in the choir. He was also determined that he would build up and coach a rugby team (Charterhouse was a football school) and perhaps even manage to beat the famous Dulwich College rugby team.

L, at school with him at the time, later wrote:

But when I think of Mark I also think of walking into his room to find him practising the cello, exposing a much more graceful and gentler side. He was truly talented when it came to music. He had a music scholarship, but that was not why he played. I recall him complaining bitterly when he had to give up evenings for orchestra practice. However, when he was playing on his own, in his room or above the South African cloisters, that was when you could see how he really thrived on his talent, extracting serenity and joy from every bow movement and sound.

Mark described the rugby team in jest as 'the worst rugby team I have ever played in'. N, who played in it with him, wrote to me after his death:

I have vivid memories of him acting like a terrier at scrum half, always chivvying and leading the pack. He was a brave guy, happy to take on and tackle people who were substantially bigger than him, on the odd occasion that he came off worse, he would pick himself up with a wry smile, and get back on with the job! He moved seamlessly between the social castes at school, never discriminating against those who others might have seen as less 'cool'. He treated all people equally, and was one of the friendliest and most lively people I have ever had the pleasure to come across.

By now he had learned to embrace physical challenge, and in 1998, only weeks before his A-level examinations, he ran the London Marathon in three hours and fourteen minutes. Of course I thought he should be working. I took him to the hospital afterwards to have his feet bandaged and take delivery of crutches.

Boarding school was the making of him as he was able to feel his own way. I would go down to see him at weekends, taking him for lunch at our beloved RHS Garden Wisley or to Pizza Express in Godalming, me worrying about the number of his activities and distractions from academic work. It was then that our relationship changed. A mother knows her child; from now he could choose what to tell me. I was aware of my boy growing up, the creeping mystery of now never really knowing the whole. I could see him slowly emerging from his chrysalis, a charming person toughened by his earlier adversity and by two years at boarding school, but still so young. We were both thinkers and talkers, and so slowly we developed an adult relationship, crafted over tables in cafés or in the outdoors together. We often spoke about the current issues in his life, solutions, just as later we would talk about how to look after his soldiers and deal with their problems.

Mark took his A-levels young at sixteen, and despite his new freedom gained good grades in two of them, the next year having to retake a third subject at a crammer in central London. He lived at home that year but seemed forever away, sleeping on floors elsewhere as I worried about him let loose on the city.

I encouraged him not to be in a hurry to go to university – again I was influenced by Winston Churchill and his belief that one should not go until one is ready. Mark was still growing (as he did until he was twenty-two, making up for his developmental delay earlier), and I felt he needed more life experience before university and his working twenties. So I suggested that he apply for an Army Gap Year Commission. After a tough live-in assessment by the Army, he passed the Army Regular Commissions Board officer selection entry to Royal Military Academy Sandhurst; however, he just failed the Gap Year Commission because of his relative youth. They said that he could take up the Sandhurst place at any time.

Instead, for this second gap year in 2001 he decided to become a jackaroo (learning farm hand) on a huge 145,000-acre outback sheep property, 'Mungadal' in Hay, NSW, Australia, managed by my second cousin. He had to survive as a pale and soft-skinned Pom in a tough country, where an English education and a veneer of sophistication did not matter. The outback lads took him as he was: they saw him think and pull his weight, become one of a team. He was flown around the property to get his bearings when he arrived, and the next day he had to go out on his motorbike to pull sheep out of a muddy waterhole, alone and a long way from the homestead. This particular day was a seminal experience for him, important enough to mention to me many thousands of miles away.

He loved the new oldness of this dry faded country. He watched fascinated whilst muscled New Zealand shearers robbed the sheep of their fleece in minutes: they then scampered away thin-coated and pink, their job done for now. But weeks later Mark had to cut off their balls and tails.

As well as his first steady girlfriend – a local trainee vet – he had a motorbike to drive around the property and his dog, all his first trappings of adulthood. He was given a weekly local radio programme, 'The Pom in Hay', and became the Hay correspondent for his journalist uncle's drive-home radio programme in Melbourne, 300 miles away. He played rugby for the Hay Cutters, and has an award still displayed in a Hay pub. He loved it, and when he came back to the UK he was serious when he suggested that I sell up and buy a property in Australia with him as the manager. He was very impressed by the straightforwardness of the Australian country lads, their relaxed, tough and honest way of life.

Rather reluctantly, Mark came home in 2002 to go to Oxford Brookes University to study Estate Management.

Whilst still in Australia he asked me to sort out his accommodation at Oxford Brookes since he could not be back in time. I remember that week so clearly. On the Thursday Elizabeth graduated from Cambridge, and we had strawberries and wine on the lawns of the Fellows' Garden surrounded by those most graceful wide borders. The next day I was at Oxford Brookes trying to decide between tatty flat after tatty flat as there was not enough first year accommodation for students. Of course, I chose wrongly, but weeks later he was able to make good when he moved in with friends.

Mark lived in a number of houses with various friends over his university years. He had a wonderful time. This was an era of outrageous behaviour for all, testing limits, seeing what they could do, and those friendships remained very powerful. After his death several wrote to me: his friend A commented that 'his true living of life is so worthy of every celebration', P reflected on 'the remarkable effect that Mark had on everyone he met' and said that 'he died a man who had achieved so much in a short space of time'. M wrote:

He had an aura about him that would light up the dullest of rooms when he walked in, an energy that made him the biggest person there: he did not have to be the loudest person, he was too laid back for that, but he had a sense of mischief and a love of life that was infectious to all around him.

Much later, several wrote to me calling him their friend, even their best friend, their mate. He was such good company – one did not mind that he was so shared because he gave so much. Perhaps it was his humility or his 'selflessness', as one friend described it. Some of those friends continued to support me after his death, helping me with the emotional task of sorting out his effects, having dinner together regularly, inviting me to their weddings.

During his years at university Mark usually took part-time jobs during his holidays to keep himself financially stable, putting down dance floors or working as a waiter. He commented to me once that one gets bigger tips if one gives people what they want – perhaps another lesson in life. He noticed thoughtfully how people responded to those serving them, some respectfully and some with disdain.

Four years later, Mark finally graduated with a degree, despite apparently little academic effort on his part. The time at university there had been important to him, allowing him to make that great leap from childhood to adulthood, to be free and have fun. Oxford Brookes seemed a very human institution, respectful of its students and wanting to bring out the best in them despite any difficulties, and I was impressed by it.

I had been aware of Mark's first stirrings with girls whilst he was at boarding school, spotty, small and thin, just beginning the long stretch of growing into a man.

He shyly had a first girlfriend, whom he then clumsily pushed into a ditch, unsure of himself and unaware of male courtesy. I was told that he jumped out of the first-floor window of a girl's bedroom; the penalty for being caught there was expulsion from school.

In his second year at university he left a message: would I ring him? I was expecting perhaps a failed exam, a request for a loan. Instead, proudly and very excitedly, he told me that G had agreed to go out with him. This was the beginning of his first long-term relationship, with a very caring pretty girl. He said to me once that 'you do not know how nice it is to wake up with an attractive girl in your bed'. He was twenty-two, and along with a steady girlfriend he had his Jack Russell bitch, Nutmeg, a small, energetic, and entertaining friend; his battered old car; and his moped, which soon became two fast motorbikes.

We bought a house in Oxford together, also his pride and joy. I helped with the deposit, he borrowed most of the money and I guaranteed the loan. We were now, rather dangerously, in business together, but it was a fruitful and cooperating working relationship with strict rules. He had a house to look after, and that taught him many lessons.

He continued to show an intuitive interest in personal, mental and physical development, jogging the Pilgrim's Way in France and north Spain with Sholto over three weeks in 2006.

Mark had an old dream, to be the youngest person to go the South Pole unaided, and in 2006 he decided to try to realise it. The year before he had been given some funding by a generous Old Carthusian living in California after writing about his dream in the school magazine, *The Carthusian* – the article showed him dragging a tyre tied to his waist as he ran uphill. With the money granted he spent ten days doing 'survival training' with Geoff Somers on the freezing tundra of Norway, building an igloo and training on the wild wasteland of the glaciers in sub-zero temperatures. He was teased by friends, who pointed out that Norway was north and the South Pole south – was he going the wrong way? He had to abandon the South Pole expedition unsuccessfully trying to raise the £90,000 in funding required.

He stopped seeing his long-term girlfriend, wanting to experiment, to be a free young man. He began to see others, all lovely girls, as this now handsome charming young man gained confidence. He was determined not to become too involved then – that would be unfair as he was about to go to Afghanistan – but he was clearly tempted. When he commented to me that he had met one girl in particular at the 'wrong time' and I suggested tentatively that he commit now, he was cross with me, accusing me of wanting him married.

As mother and son, we were close and shared an important part of ourselves. Like me, he loved gardening and constructing our new garden from its derelict beginnings. When he was a teenager we would often watch gardening programmes together. I remember an episode of *Gardeners' World* about setting up a compost heap – despite many replays of the video we ended up falling about laughing as we were unable to decide whether it needed to be laced with tea or pee, as instructed by Bob Flowerdew with his ponytail.

We recognised and understood some of the same in the other: our sensitivity to people, wanting to make things better, our sociability. When the front door bell rang on a Friday evening and I could see his slight frame through the glass of the door, I knew I was about to have a very good time for a couple of hours. The right size frame at the door would remind me of him for a long time. This adult son was now very kind and caring to me, although also firm and quite demanding that I had to try, be fit, look after myself, no self-indulgence. The year before he died we climbed in the Black Mountains together, and he pressured me not to let a younger group overtake. I was in my sixties but nevertheless required to compete, to do more than my best.

We went to Australia and Bali together just weeks before he left to go to Afghanistan. I heard later from a friend of his that he had been committed to going skiing with his mates for those same two weeks and had reneged, to their irritation, to come with me to see the family in Australia instead, perhaps for one last time. He did not tell me about the skiing holiday. On that trip, for the first time I saw the mature and adult young man he had become, able to handle social situations confidently and sensitively. Previously, I had taken him on holiday; this time he seemed to take me, making sure that I could deal with what came our way. When I nagged about putting on suntan lotion in the hot Australian sun he chided me: did I not know that he was responsible for looking after a whole platoon? I became aware of his fitness, his more mature body now muscled and solid as he did press-ups or jogged along Palm Beach. This time, unusually for him, he asked me to photograph him more often; he seemed to want me to have a record if necessary. I could now see a person to be respected, an adult able and wanting to put aside childish things.

We parted at Hong Kong airport. He had no money and he was cross that I fretted about this as he left to visit a friend. Later, he was fairly non-committal about his weekend there, except to mention its fun and a speedboat. After his death, a girl wrote to me who had spent the night with him, a beautiful, honest and thoughtful letter. To me this letter was a symbol of his caring generation, a girl reaching out to the mother of a man she had just met at a party, both at the time fancy-free:

It was a shock to know that he had died and I wanted to let you know that although I only knew him for one night I will remember him and miss him regardless of how brief it was. He had such an effect on me. I would have loved to be able to have had more time with him but feel privileged I got to meet him at all.

Sadly the brightness of his life contrasted with the awfulness of his death only weeks later.

CHAPTER 4

THE ARMY

One day in December 2008 a letter had arrived. It was Mark's writing on a battered envelope, and inside was a photocopy of a typed report. It was his latest, and in fact last, report from the Welsh Guards. Scrawled on the back in pencil, he had written, 'Impressed?'

The report read:

Lt Evison is an exceptionally impressive officer. He is bright, positive, fit, robust and charismatic. He is at home in the field but smart in the barracks. Importantly, he is set apart from his contemporaries because he combines real talent with great humility and charm. He also maintains many interests outside the Army and he is a talented musician.

Lt Evison has had an outstanding start to his career in the Army. He arrived at 1 WG [1st Battalion Welsh Guards] with an A grade from PCD [Platoon Commanders Division] having finished as one of the top officers on the course. He has excelled in everything that has been asked of him during a demanding year and he was particularly impressive in BATUS [British Army

Training Unit Suffield, Canada] and Germany. The US Army, who acted as Observer Controllers in Germany, singled him out as a very capable platoon commander and his soldiers have nicknamed him '007', which whilst humorous, does indicate their respect for his ability. He cares deeply about his men and takes great trouble to ensure that they never want for anything. He has healthy relationships with his NCOs [Non-Commissioned Officers] but he must guard against familiarity.

Lt Evison is the best platoon commander in my company, and he is also the most junior. His men are fortunate to have him as a commander ... Lt Evison displays more potential than any young officer with whom I have worked. His manner, intellect and tactical acumen, combined with his humility, bode well for a notable military future. He should be promoted to captain at the very earliest opportunity.

Lt Evison must be given demanding and interesting appointments. In the short term, he would be outstanding as OC [Officer in Charge] Guards Parachute Platoon (3 PARA) for which I give him the strongest recommendation; he would represent all that is best about the Household Division, but is suitably robust to hold his own, and more, in the Parachute regiment. His medium term goal is UK SF [Special Forces] selection where I suspect he will give an impressive performance.

Longer term, Lt Evison is a must for a key Battalion staff appointment (Adjt, Ops Offr or IO) [Adjutant,

Operations Officer or Intelligence Officer] and he has the makings of an outstanding Rifle Company Commander. He is a must for conversion to his commission.

I was indeed impressed. As a mother, one carries in one's mind always the boy, and this boy always the naughty boy. I could forget for now his lukewarm school reports, his detentions; a talent just not yet alight. This naughty boy had somehow become a leader of men and his promise was acknowledged here by his new masters. And this was also a career rather than operational forecast.

The Army was Mark's adult life. That is where he blossomed, became a man. His natural talents – thinking quickly on his feet, his affection for others, his 'great heart' and charm, his physical fitness, discipline and love of adventuring – all found an outlet there. It was made for him and he loved it.

Why did Mark join the Army? One looks for seeds, those small influences on young minds searching for direction. As a teenager in the Dulwich College Combined Cadet Force, Mark won Best Cadet in 1996 and Best Gunner in 1997, and I had noticed the relish with which he squirmed through the mud, how much he enjoyed it. Perhaps it goes back even earlier. When he was a young cub, small and blond and fast as quicksilver, he was awarded the Cub Scout Challenge, the first of his Cub Scouts group to gain such an award, and so given to him by an important commissioner. About the same age, he lost himself in the summer hedgerows of south London, wandering away too far, always wanting to go and explore, to push on further. When we walked up steep hills on holiday he would run to the top and back again, there and back twice whilst we struggled on. His father took him on camping and walking holidays as a teenager, to Hadrian's Wall, the Peak District. They both loved the outdoors, the rolling views, the cool clear air, the freedom of it.

Another influence may have been boarding school, when at sixteen he sang as a chorister in the Charterhouse chapel every Sunday. It is a graceful and elegant building, built to honour old Carthusians who died in the First World War and described there as the largest war memorial in the UK. The school song is 'Jerusalem' – that most beautiful poem by Blake put to Sir Hubert Parry's rousing music in 1916, which was taken to signify individuality and freedom of thought, the prize of the Great War, and then the Suffrage movement. Its last stanzas he would have sung many times:

> Bring me my Bow of burning gold;
> Bring me my Arrows of desire:
> Bring me my Spear: O clouds unfold!
> Bring me my Chariot of fire!
> I will not cease from Mental Fight,
> Nor shall my Sword sleep in my hand:
> Till we have built Jerusalem,
> In England's green and pleasant Land

Rousing and patriotic stuff for young men. I could never hear that hymn again without weeping.

So in 2007 Mark decided to take up the place at RMA Sandhurst he had been offered four years before. He wanted his adventuring, his travel, his skiing and climbing, perhaps even a trip to the South Pole, and he thought the Army might give him that. But he was ambitious and practical also and knew that even if he was not happy there, the Army would give him personal development training, teach him skills he could use later in life, perhaps in another career. He understood, possibly, that for him to sit still at a desk all day would be tough: maybe later. At the time he made the choice he had been at home, restless after university, energetic, wanting to grow up and embrace life. This time he would enjoy the teaching and training, it would play to his strengths. So he chose the Army.

Sandhurst, that 200-year-old bastion of British heroism and leadership, brought out a seriousness in Mark, a sense of responsibility for others which I had occasionally seen in him before but which now became more central, made his life more meaningful. In a sense, the teaching there coincided with my view that challenge pushed one on and made one bigger, any challenge, and that difficult experiences shape and teach. I watched as he became bigger, more confident, more thoughtful.

He told me that those very demanding first three months at Sandhurst were intended to weed out the uncertain, the doubters. There was no home leave and intense difficult training for the new tissue-soft recruits. He found those weeks a strain but he did not complain to me. I was surprised that he managed the polishing, cleaning, marching, ironing, taking orders from tough shouting colour sergeants, the conformity of it. It was the preparation of young innocent people for the ravages of war, inuring them early and fast to its potential brutality, teaching them to fight, to kill. Hammering them into what they all wanted to be, officers in the British Army.

Sandhurst taught these young people to lead from the front, to put duty and sacrifice ahead of even one's own life. It was to be unlimited obligation beyond the boundary of life, so that in battle having to give your life for your men was second nature, no need for further thought. There was an emphasis there on somehow preparing for that one necessary moment. The recruits learned to be the inspiration as well as the support for their platoon, to consider the needs of all, to lead by serving. They were idealistic and wanting adventure. When war actually came, some left soon after, turning against it, shocked.

I did not allow myself to think about the dangers of Mark joining the Army. It was his choice, and so I fretted and nagged him about his motorbikes instead. I did ask him if he would be able to kill, but by then he had been at Sandhurst for that first difficult term and seemed almost conditioned to accept it, even desensitised to death and what it meant. But I knew that he would be thoughtful about the morality of killing, that he was too intelligent to manage blind patriotism. His father is a pacifist, living in a country where the wounds of war have turned generations afterwards against it. But Mark was aware of the horror and pain of terrorism; he had cycled through the streets immediately after the London bombings in 2005. There were pressures on him to come to terms with death and killing, from Sandhurst and from his experiences. They had to do it; it was part of their new job.

His diary, kept whilst at Sandhurst, showed a young puppy of a man changing into a serious young adult:

I handed in my war studies essay on Monday and am awaiting my mark with anticipation. For the first time in my academic career I have worked hard at this essay to the extent of handing in two drafts, finishing the essay early in order to proofread it and researching properly using books from the library. My character must be changing to a certain extent. What I have also noticed is that my alertness has increased by a huge amount – I feel awake all the time and have huge amounts of energy. I put this down to a combination of physical exercise and limited sleep – 8 hours or less is all I need now compared to the 10+ I was having at university. Less sleep also allows you to do more during the day.

The Sandhurst diary shows his growing will to do well, and a frustration with himself if he let himself down. He says about an exercise: 'To those who do not care that is not a problem, however I would like to do fairly well – mostly for pride.'

This was a very different Mark. He worked and began to show signs of becoming tidy and disciplined. And, as always, he had fun.

A letter written to me after his death by a Sandhurst friend summarises Mark then:

The second reason I was writing was to try and tell you about the side of Mark that I knew and how we first met.

I remember seeing Mark a couple of times during our initial few days at Sandhurst. You see we were in the same platoon and went through training together up until the point where I got injured in training at Brecon. On initial impressions of Mark I remember thinking to myself that he was a good bloke and definitely someone I wanted to get to know. He had that effect on people. When you met him, you just wanted to be in his company and be mates with him. He is genuinely one of the few people I have met who has had that effect. We didn't get to be properly good mates till we spent a week together on AT [adventure training] in Wales. The week would have been intensely boring were it not for Mark. He and I would go on drives around the countryside in the evenings or go fishing. We would normally end up with a crate of beer chatting on the beach having a lot of banter with our other mate.

Mark was a great one for the banter. Once he put a dead squirrel in my sock drawer just before an inspection. Luckily I found it in time! He was also incredibly fit. He never seemed to struggle at Sandhurst. When I was knackered and beginning to fall behind I would find him at my side encouraging me along. He would always be one of the guys others would go to if they needed a bit of help and he always made time for you.

When we went to Oman together, we all went out drinking, which is fairly dodgy in a Muslim country. By the end of the night we all found ourselves in a position where we were surrounded by several policemen. I ended up getting handcuffed and taken to a Middle Eastern police cell. Not an enviable position. Everyone else had legged it, apart from Mark, who made his own way down to the police station and managed to talk them into letting me go. My brief stint in the Army would have been over it if it weren't for him.

I have a lot to thank your son for. His friendship and loyalty being key. When he found out he was going to the Welsh Guards he was so happy. Out of everybody that I knew at Sandhurst he really found his niche in not only being in the Army but also the regiment. He loved soldiering and his boys. He loved being in the Welsh Guards and always lived his life to the fullest.

I was in Afghanistan in Nad-e-Ali in the same area as Mark in 2008. It was a tough environment to be in. When I came back, he and I would chat for ages about it. He was one of the first people to greet me on my return and helped me settle into life again. I know he did his boys proud out there and that they all loved him as we did.

Mark chose the Welsh Guards as his regiment: he was drawn to them and they to him. After working together as a team on exercise these Welsh soldiers laughed, talked, shared their feelings, sang and played rugby together, a powerful mix for Mark. They called themselves a family – they were brothers, working together, looking after each other. They became very close in difficult circumstances, each dependent on the other, with space only for cooperation and not for competition. As a regiment they have ceremonial duties, and Mark told me with some relish how he had eaten off gold plate whilst supervising stiff soldiers in bearskins at Buckingham Palace. It was another world for him.

So Mark became a young lieutenant in charge of 7 Platoon, attached to Number 3 Company of the Welsh Guards commanded by Major Guy Stone.

The Welsh Guards obituary, published in their magazine, explained his next eighteen months for me:

After the mandatory platoon commanders course at Brecon, where he was awarded an A grade with a recommendation to return as an instructor, Mark's first year in the battalion was, as it always is, frenetic. A battlefield tour of Normandy with the regiment's old and bold was followed by the Queen's Birthday Parade and then exercises in Canada and Germany. Training for the deployment to Afghanistan started in earnest in the autumn of 2008 and his platoon flourished. His guardsmen realised that they had an outstanding leader and that they would be in good hands for the forthcoming tour.

Mark emailed me during this time, on 17 September 2008:

Dear Mum,

All fine here, we have finished the live firing package and have moved onto the counter insurgency part where they have flown 400 Afghan nationals, none of which speak English, and moved them into three purpose-built villages so that we can get as realistic training as possible – amazing really.

My foot has now pretty much recovered which is good. No real other news. The platoon is working really well and it will be a pleasure to take them away next year – some real characters!

He cared about those men in his platoon, worried about their wellbeing. Their fears he made his fears as he worried about how they would cope, whether they would abscond before they left for war, how he would keep up their morale.

After he died, Mark's soldiers told me about his

professionalism, his cool head under pressure, his tactical awareness, his setting an example and wanting them to be the best platoon. They were the ones who, under his leadership, agreed to wade through a river whilst on exercise when the platoon was given the choice to stay dry. One exercise in Scotland began with being offloaded fully clothed through a bitterly cold, angry northern sea, and then two weeks' damp survival in dark Scottish forests. Afterwards, his Army report singled out his positive attitude, how he approached even the most demoralising of tasks with a smile, how he tried to help others. That was Mark.

At the time he went to Sandhurst, Afghanistan was only a possibility, not a certainty. Later, when he knew where he was going, he seemed cautious about it. Like most, or all, at Sandhurst, he must have thought that ultimate danger – death or serious injury – was going to happen to the other guy. He worried about it and worked at his fitness, knowing that this might protect him. He said to a friend that if they did a very good job they would survive. But fate and luck are no respecters of effort.

In Helmand, Mark's 7 Platoon were now to be 'seconded' to Number 2 Company under the leadership of Major Henry Bettinson. Major Guy Stone was to mentor the ANA (Afghan National Army) soldiers with the remainder of Number 3 Company in Sangin. The Welsh Guards battle group was to be under the overall command of Lieutenant Colonel Rupert Thorneloe, operating from an 'ops room' at Bastion. They were just one of several battle groups who together made up the 19th Brigade, a huge tranche of about 6,000 soldiers under Brigadier Tim Radford, with headquarters in Lashkar Gah.

Mark had met Brigadier Radford at a 'fireside chat' briefing in the Welsh Guards barracks at Aldershot. Mark was sufficiently impressed to tell me about the evening. Brigadier Radford had underlined the need for leadership and resilience; he must have understood their potential vulnerability, as he spoke of the importance of this part of Helmand for the whole campaign, that it may even be won and lost in this tour.

Fifteen months after leaving Sandhurst, and after many months of training with 7 Platoon, Mark said goodbye at our front door and, hours later, arrived in southern Helmand province, Afghanistan. He had been given one of the most difficult postings: the turreted fort Haji-Alem near Nad-e-Ali. It was one of three patrol bases that the Welsh Guards had taken over in 2009. They were fairly close to one another – Haji-Alem, Tanda and Paraang – and each housed a platoon led by a young lieutenant. This was to be home for six months for the men. They were behind enemy lines, and Mark described it to a girlfriend as 'the most dangerous place on earth'.

I had very little information about how it was for him, except for emails, letters and that one longer phone call. But clearly he and the other soldiers were enjoying themselves. Deep in Afghanistan, in that small dirty dusty patrol base for six months, their human need for closeness must somehow have been almost completely satisfied: a strange primal experience, living, fighting and laughing together, proving themselves to each other, males in a pack, only simple comforts. Testosterone, fear, anxiety, anger, adrenalin raised man against man. It is what they were trained to do, but it was also more. Perhaps it was living the war movie rather than watching it – the dust, the pain, the danger. Years after, in retirement or with a deskbound job in London, Army men will often long for that time, that closeness, that fun, that unselfishness.

Before Mark left London, a friend had given him a journal as a goodbye present. She knew that he had been typing up his grandfather's diary, written longhand about his time as a missionary in China from 1937 to 1950. It was a detailed and fascinating account of the time, a potent story of loneliness, uncertainty, strange ways and, eventually, danger. Mark had been impressed by its fingers into times past, its simple and elegant writing style.

Thus he began this first posting with this new diary, which can be seen in a photograph of him at the patrol base, laid out with his few things amongst the very basic kit in his corner, his Army hammock and net. It recorded his experience from the time of leaving home and arriving in Kandahar airport to just before he died. It is a moving account of how it was there, written with the flies and heat of Afghanistan around him. It some ways it is also a lonely account, a diary written to give him solace, helping him direct his thoughts as the only officer there, in command.

The fighting Army is an eminently practical organisation. Soldiers are doing what they have been told to do by the government and by politicians, as well as they know how and with whatever they are given. But of course they think about the rights and wrongs of the wars and conflicts they fight: an experienced lieutenant-colonel later said to me that he would be happy if no shots were fired during his forthcoming tour. Mark was to observe, and the journal was where he put his thoughts.

CHAPTER 5

MARK'S JOURNAL

On Thursday 9 July 2009, two months after Mark's death, almost concurrently two important things happened, very significant in the later scheme of things.

A package was delivered to me at home by the Army, which I had been told was Mark's personal diary. It was a warm summer day and I sat in my garden room, the package next to me on the sofa.

As I sat there, the telephone rang. It was a producer from *Newsnight*. My name had been suggested as a person who might speak about 'the human cost' of the Afghanistan conflict with Jeremy Paxman the following Monday. Would I think of doing it? I was non-committal, my life had changed. I was asked for my views, which I tried to explain: I had accepted that we were fighting in Afghanistan because we were fighting terrorism, that the war prevented further terrorism here, and that we were dealing with other issues as well, the drugs trade to the UK and women's rights. Mark had died doing his job and 'serving his country'. I mentioned that this package was next to me, as yet unopened; the producer wanted to know more about it. She said she would ring me back to confirm.

Inside the package was Mark's diary. The moment felt very slow and surreal – this was my boy writing his thoughts, his fingers had held these pages. It was a beautiful book, cased in brown leather and with yellow-ish paper, and inside was even, tidy, thoughtful pencilled writing, nothing crossed out, no second thoughts. It was to tell me about Mark and how he was until two days before he died. He would not have imagined the impact it would have, on me and on the world back home, even unfinished as it was.

I rang my partner John and read parts to him. John realised the political implications of it immediately – the diary of a dead soldier no longer bound by the strictures of Army codes. It had been written as a private journal, never intended to be seen by the world, not to be published, so its integrity could not be questioned. Mark had no personal axe to grind, no ulterior motive when he wrote, it was what he saw, how he felt. There were even a few highly personal parts that were not for other eyes. I was confused about what I should do. In some ways it felt too private to let the general public see, and yet I thought I had a duty to make it available so that others could read it, and so that, in the future, historians could use it as source material. I contacted a friend, a journalist with the *Daily Telegraph* who had known Mark since childhood, and read parts of the diary to him. He arranged for me to see his editor the following day.

The next day I had been invited to a lunch with the Club Secretary and some Welsh Guards officers at the Cavalry and Guards Club in Piccadilly, where Mark had been a member and where his name was to be put in their Book of Remembrance. I mentioned the diary: had it been read? I was anxious about crossing a line; it seemed to me to be a potentially controversial document and I did not want to compromise the Welsh Guards, partly because of Mark's love for the regiment and also for the Army. In fact it had been read by an officer who was there at lunch and who was in charge of co-ordinating the arrival of Welsh Guards war dead at Wootton Bassett Air Force base. He made no comment when I said I was visiting the *Daily Telegraph* that afternoon. I took this to be his silent ratifying of its publication, perhaps its roots in his concern about what he had seen.

I met the *Telegraph* editor that afternoon. She showed considerable interest in the diary, offering a generous sum for its publication, which we insisted should be for the benefit of the Mark Evison Foundation, the charity we had recently set up. She, John and Sholto handled all the legal aspects of publishing, drafting agreements, copyright issues and world-wide syndication.

Two days later it was confirmed: I would appear on *Newsnight* the following Monday in a programme titled 'Afghanistan, the Human Cost' with Jeremy Paxman.

My old public shyness had by now been swallowed up by a profound sense of irrelevance, nothing mattered except death. I could no longer see a reason not to do an interview; on the other hand, there were some reasons to do it. I could say what I knew to the public because clearly others wanted to hear and understand. I was now aware of the needs of the soldiers who had brought Mark back to the patrol base and then had to fight on, and I wanted to try to help them and make things better, in my own tiny way, for all those fighting in Helmand. Mark was on my shoulder.

Before the *Newsnight* appearance I was told that the MOD attempted to stop me appearing because I was 'angry' about Mark's death; the Welsh Guards reassured them that I was not. This was the first time I was personally aware of the MOD's pressure and it felt inappropriate, an effort to control me when it was not necessary. It was perhaps to augur what was ahead.

I was interviewed three times that Monday: by *Newsnight* and *Daily Telegraph* journalists at home and then in the evening by Jeremy Paxman. I met him as I was 'made up', and he remained courteous throughout, thoughtful and considerate. I was then ushered into a tiny room with others, all invited for their very differing views. It was tense with expectation as we all tried to say little to one another, perhaps expecting controversy, perhaps not wanting to explain ourselves too soon. Then it was my turn and I walked into the studio, the bright lights everywhere. I decided to try to speak slowly, to allow the audience and me time. As is the custom on the programme, we were not warned of questions and so I had to think as I spoke, demanding for a first television appearance. I began tired, it was late, and after it I was exhausted. It was a surreal experience as I sensed people across the country watching in their living rooms, perhaps millions of them. But as at the funeral I chose to deal with this very public experience by reminding myself that these were friends, they were on my side, there for me. That helped.

Jeremy Paxman asked me finally if I thought Mark's death had been for a worthy cause. I said that as a mother I could think of nothing worthy enough to counter a son's death, but that being a soldier had been Mark's choice, he loved the Army, it was his call. Afterwards I was very pleased that other mourning mothers contacted me to tell me I had spoken for them. I did not like how I presented when I saw a replay afterwards, but others seemed to.

Mark's slightly redacted diary was then published in the *Daily Telegraph* the next day, 14 July. It was printed over three pages of the newspaper with a photograph of Mark looking handsome in his uniform on the front page.

So many people wrote to me afterwards, touching, personal letters. This profound kindness and understanding from people out there, unknown to me, was one of the most uplifting and surprising consequences of Mark's death – the powerful empathy and reaching out of strangers trying to make it better for me. Often they had been through other wars – some were elderly, they understood. They often thanked me for sharing the diary, they wanted to know.

14/07/09

Dear Mrs Evison,

I write to send you and your family our deepest sympathy in the tragic loss of your clearly wonderful son. We have been very moved by his remarkable journal and your interview, both of which are sure to have a timely impact on political attitudes.

These are difficult times both politically and militarily and even more so personally for families caught up in it. We're thinking of you.

I too have, and had, soldier sons (Irish Guards and SAS; Green Jacket and SAS). The elder, M, was Commander British Forces, Afghanistan, last year.

With best wishes to you all. No reply.

Yours sincerely, M

(Major General Sir)

And again:

17/07/09

Dear Margaret Evison,

I was very moved reading your son's journal written in Afghanistan.

He sounds so much like my own sons with so much to give and so much to live for that it is quite unbelievable that they should be gone and we are left. I know that you will be very proud of him as a man and as a soldier but I cannot help feeling that the loss of him as a son will be hard for you to bear in private. If it can be any consolation his journal has brought this war into every home in England and indeed it brought it to the forefront of our thoughts and hopefully political actions. It has made us all realise the sacrifice being made in our name and how brave these young men really are.

I am so sorry for your loss but please know that so many in the country are feeling for you and the painful loss of our dead and wounded soldiers in Afghanistan is affecting the lives of us all.

With my sincere condolences

The problem seemed simple to the press: not enough helicopters and an unsupportive Prime Minister. On 14 July 2009, just five days after I had received the package, the *Daily Telegraph* ran an article headed 'Helicopter budget cut by half since 2001'. But I was becoming aware that this was in fact only one of several important issues as outlined in Mark's diary, including poor equipment and insufficient supplies. This view had been widely promoted by General Sir Richard Dannatt, head of the Army (now Lord Dannatt), who had over the previous few years continued to highlight the poor funding, preparation and equipment available, and the wider moral issues involved in that. He had first commented publicly in a controversial interview with Sarah Sands of the *Daily Mail* on 10 October 2006 about the huge pressure it would cause the forces to be fighting on two fronts, Iraq and Afghanistan. As an older soldier with a pride in old-fashioned 'moral integrity' he was sensitive to the Military Covenant, that mutual obligation between the state and the Armed Forces that personnel can expect to be treated fairly and have the support of the nation, society and the government to sustain them whilst soldiering. He was very aware of the Army's responsibility to the men who served, especially at the front. But he was only one of three heads of the Armed Forces, and his views about priorities were diluted by other needs.

Mark's diary read as follows:

Afghanistan 2009
15 April
It is always the hardest part to start a journal. Where to begin? Should one start with feelings past or just start from the beginning. As my grandfather once said, it is best just to put pen to paper and write.

Anticipation, excitement, fear – all words which could be used to describe what one should be feeling right now but the only one that I really feel is uncertainty. I am currently sitting under neon lights of a mortar-proof marquee on Kandahar airfield. Due to this, the reality of where I am has not yet hit. The only other feeling is that of an emptiness for those that I have left behind. Goodbyes are not the easiest to deal with but one can prepare for some – mothers, sisters, fathers etc. The others are those that catch you unaware. Those that you thought were going to be easy sometimes become harder than the others. I travelled to London yesterday to sort out one final goodbye with a friend which ended up being the hardest so far. My feelings are now in turmoil.

We now fly to Camp Bastion by Hercules and then start the RSOI [reception, staging and onward integration] package tomorrow afternoon – I have been warned that it will be death by PowerPoint.

16 April

We have now moved fully into Camp Bastion and partaking in the RSOI package. This is a four day live firing package which is mandatory for all who arrive in Afghanistan. It is also a good way to acclimatise and finally try out all the kit we have been issued – including the Osprey [body armour].

Bastion is a bizarre place. It is situated in the middle of the desert with majestic mountains rising to the north and south approximately 10 km away. Apart from that it is flat and so with the addition of the HESCO [sandbag] walls which are 20 feet high gives the feeling of complete isolation within the base. It is so powerful that it does not feel like we are in a war zone and only a few km outside of the walls are people who would want to do you harm. On top of this the food is fantastic – there is a pizza hut and an internet suite which is faster than those at home.

We were on the ranges today testing our weapons and we met an old acquaintance of mine from school, X, who has just finished his sixth month tour operating as a mobile operations group around the whole of Afghanistan. When he asked where I was heading and he found out it was Nad-e-Ali he took a small step back and wished me all the best – in fact this had happened a number of times. I can only guess that this is because of two reasons. Firstly, being knowledgeable he really does know it will be tough or secondly that he has heard but is talking a big game. Either way, waiting in Bastion is not ideal as at the moment I just want to get stuck in and see for myself what it is like. How will I react with my first contact? Will I freeze or hopefully prove my worth. At the moment it is a waiting game and until that moment comes I can only speculate.

17 April

The problem with the Guards is that even when deployed they are still a stickler for rules. I was approached by the battalion second in command earlier today who stated that I should have not cut my hat down. In earnest I bought it that way and stated my case. He proceeded to walk off muttering under his breath – 'Platoon commanders these days.' It seems that they are more interested in how we look rather than the fact that as a battalion we are soon to be facing the fiercest fighting probably since the Second World War. The men seem prepared to a certain extent but whether they are there mentally will be the deciding factor. I fully expect them to refuse to soldier. If that is the case then how will I persuade them to change? It will be hard.

On a more positive note I have found the pull up bar – great success.

21 April

I have now reached the front line in the form of FOB [Forward Operating Base] Silab – approx 15 km west of Bastion in the Nad-e-Ali district. We moved out of Bastion yesterday and transported the Vikings through the desert to drop down into the Green Zone to reduce the chances of striking an IED [improvised explosive device].

The Viking vehicle was designed for use in the Scandinavian countries against attack from what was the USSR. Used extensively by the Royal Marines they have been adapted for use in the desert with different tracks, increased armour and more importantly air conditioning.

We mounted up first thing in the morning and with a few rather nervous passengers, myself included, we left. One very long hour afterwards we rolled into Silab – home for the next few days and my first taste of Afghanistan and the much talked about compounds.

It is a FOB approx 200 m by 100 m with 3 x 105 guns attached. Four sangars [sandbag fortifications] mounted 24 hours a day by both Estonians and artillery. The ops room with internet and facilities lies to the north. I have been placed in a compound further west which although it is further away from the ops room (a positive) is right next to the gun line and twice now I have jumped out of my skin as they fire with no warning.

After a day of relaxing and getting used to the difference between Bastion and the FOB I prepared myself for patrol at 0800 the following morning.

This included visiting the armoury. Unlike back in the UK where everything is accountable, here once it is handed out it is written off – essentially used up even if not fired. Another point is that here there are many more varieties of weapon systems, some I have not seen or heard of. To that extent after 15 mins in the ammo store I walked out with enough kit to start my own war, including an anti-tank weapon and two red phos grenades, as well as the standard personal ammunition.

I got an early night and caught up on some much-needed sleep.

The following morning I rose early, had breakfast and re-checked my kit ready for the 0800 leave. Having met the platoon commander and getting a brief overview of the patrol, we were to move north along a road with one section moving to the west along compounds which have been used for firing points. We were heading for Green 1, a junction of both road and canal and a point where I was told Taleban used regularly. The first twenty mins were the worst. It is the uncertainty of not knowing when it will happen which plays on your mind. Almost nothing did happen. I am sure that as soon as a contact happens, you soon forget about the sickly fear and concentrate on more important things. We held a mins' shura [consultation, meeting] with three Afghans and moved back to the FOB. It really is true that they have nothing. The children are all smiling with beautiful faces. The men are more guarded and generally stand-offish. However they are willing to talk which goes against all the briefs I have been given.

The rest of the day has been spent trying to prepare for my move into Haji-Alem, an old smuggling fort that my platoon is taking over on the 24th when they arrive. I have been trying to work out exactly what is and what is not here. This is harder than it seems. Paperwork trails which tend to disappear are commonplace. As it stands I have a lack of radios, water, food and medical equipment. This with manpower is what these missions lack. It is disgraceful to send a platoon into a very dangerous area with two weeks' water and food and one team medics pack. Injuries will be sustained which I will not be able to treat and deaths could occur which could have been stopped. We are walking on a tightrope and from what it seems here are likely to fall unless drastic measures are undertaken.

On top of this I seem to have hit a wall, feel dreadful and fear I may have a fever. I will speak to mum tonight and hopefully this will cheer me up. I need an early night ready to move out at 0900 tomorrow with the Estonians.

26 April

Haji-Alem. This is the name of the fort that my platoon are now occupying. It was built fairly recently but to the design of an old fort. It is therefore very defendable – four turrets on each corner give excellent views to all compass points and being the tallest building in Nad-e-Ali it is quite imposing.

The platoon moved in three days ago, however I only joined them last night. This was because of the fever I had caught days previously. I did move with the Estonians early the morning of the 22nd but after I had reached Haji-Alem and conducted a two hour patrol with the then platoon commander I was in all sorts of trouble and so had to move back to Silab with them to recover for a few days leaving X in charge of the platoon.

The fever has hit fairly hard – cold sweats, aching limbs and headaches. More importantly it has stopped my appetite and so over the last two days the weight has just fallen off. Now that I am better I need to build this weight up by eating as much as possible. I have been forced to read Jeffrey Archer which I have always vowed

I would not. In earnest it is not too bad. He writes well and his stories are imaginative and flow easily.

Whilst I was recovering in Silab, X took the platoon on their first patrol. To the SW of Haji-Alem are well known Taleban compounds. A place one would not venture to with soldiers who have not been out on the ground and do not know the combat indicators, these come with time etc. He then patrolled towards these compounds at the hottest point of the day. He sustained a heat casualty (who had just come off 5 hours of stag [duty]) and due to this was lucky enough not to walk into an ambush. As it was the patrol was contacted whilst moving back with the heat injury and managed to mortally wound a civilian who died back in Bastion after presenting himself at Haji-Alem and being extracted.

I can only think of two reasons why he would have led the patrol in the direction he did. Firstly, and more believable, he is the Command 2 i/c [company second in command], whose main job over the next few months will be watch keeping or making sure the ops room runs smoothly. This was his opportunity to say that he had fought in Afghanistan and has fired back at the enemy. The second reason could be quite simply that he is incompetent. His route selection moving to and from the compound could definitely explain this, he was moving across raised open ground with well-known firing points only 33 m away across a poppy field. Whatever the reason is, he risked quite a lot more than I think he knew.

I am now sitting on radio stag at 0645 with another glorious Afghan day beating down on us. Not one cloud in the sky. I wonder if they appreciate what a change it is to the normal grey British climate, I doubt it. The fort is now fairly sorted. There are showers (1 a week), a chill out area with BBQ (nothing yet to cook) and a gym. The loos are fairly basic with just a hole in the ground for pissing and an ammo tin for turds which must be burnt by the unfortunate individual who fills it up. We could be here for six months and so it is good to get it up and running to a good standard so the boys can relax etc.

It is good being back. The platoon cheered me when I turned up and so for some strange reason I think they must have missed me.

27 April

The heat out here is something I have never experienced in my life. Both Oman and Morocco, although being of similar intensity, feel different. The sun here is just so powerful. By 0900 the sun is already fairly high in the sky and the power is staggering. The hottest part is between 1100 and 1400 and then it suddenly drops and is relatively cool by 1700. I think this can be put down to both altitude and the closeness to the equator. Added to the proximity of the walls within the fort and we have a living oven. There is no respite and it seems the shade makes no difference.

So we have been confined to the fort for the last two days. Two reasons for this, firstly our ECM [electronic counter measure] is down and secondly we have been restricted by the commanding officer to patrol out to a maximum distance of 200 m. We are to wait until we have an interpreter with the Icom [radio system/scanner] before we can push out further.

On a positive, this gives the platoon time to get used to the heat whilst on small patrols.

We received our first livestock this morning. Sgt X managed using sign language to persuade a local to sell us a turkey for the bargain price of $25. The only problem which could prove to be fairly major is that at the moment 'Terry' as the boys have named him seems both adverse to biscuit brown and biscuit fruit. We aim to put him on the BBQ next Sunday night but we don't want him to lose weight so it might have to be done earlier. Also on that vein how to do the deed – it would seem a little unfair to shoot him and so a knife seems the likely alternative.

At the moment life is great.

28 April

Frustration and boredom is now beginning to kick in. Frustration at not being able to push out as I know I can and boredom for the boys who are spending most of their time on stag. The poppy harvest is still ongoing and so the Taleban are quiet. They are waiting. If they attack us now they know we will retaliate and they run the risk of alienating the local population. Today two families were seen moving N to S in two vehicles full of kit. This is probably due to the poppy harvest coming to the end but it could be because the Taleban have told them to move out of the area.

The boys are also beginning to get quite jumpy. With long periods of quiet I expect this is very normal. Soldiers will want to get out there and not allow their imaginations get the better of them. The sniper and javelin pairs seem to be itching to get their respective weapons employed. I seem to be the only one here who believes that war might not be the answer to this particular problem. We must work on relationships with the Afghanis if we are to build a future for them. Maybe my perspective will change in the next few days and weeks.

30 April

The first casualty. Yesterday morning at 1048 Sgt Fasfous an MFC [mortar fire controller] was on patrol with an OMLT [operational mentor and liaison team] in a joint patrol with an ANA north of Gereshk. The callsign was contacted and unfortunately he was killed instantly as well as one interpreter. A captain in the Light Dragoons was seriously injured and extracted by MERT [medical emergency response team] to Bastion.

It is a blow for the Welsh Guards. He was a very well respected and professional Lance Sgt and will be sorely missed. Breaking the news to the boys was hard. I think reality has now really hit home. X, a childhood friend, has taken the news badly and will need to be monitored closely over the next few days to make sure he is OK. It's strange to think that I was talking to him only a couple of weeks ago. Life is fragile and out here it feels like it can be removed in an instant. It almost makes life even more valuable and shows the fragility that many in the West I believe do not understand.

We are now fully up and running within the fort. We received ten ANA soldiers this morning, with an interpreter and Icom scanner. This makes my life a lot easier and a lot more interesting.

I joined them for a lunch of boiled rice and discussed how they can be integrated within the platoon whilst on patrol. Already in the few hours they have been here they have pushed out to the neighbouring compounds. The locals are very happy we are here and have given a steer as to where they believe the Taleban to be. The SW is where we will patrol tomorrow and where they believe the Taleban to be.

The biggest fear I have whilst in the fort for six months is keeping the morale up of the men. Currently we have a satellite phone but as it stands, no way of charging it. On top of that, the CLP [combat logistic patrol] that arrived today did so without the post which was expected. The company members in Silab with internet terminals and two satellite phones must understand that currently the largest source of morale is from post. All iPods have run out of battery and to arrive with no post is inexcusable. It is a hard life in these forward PBs [patrol bases] and we need all the morale we can get. We are running a fines book which brings the platoon together every night. It is a great way of keeping up morale and hopefully by the end of the tour we should have enough money for a great night out on the platoon.

The ANA are an interesting bunch. They earn $200 a month, compared to what they could do if they farmed poppies, $4,000 a month. Many of them fight for blood feuds with the Taleban who have killed various family members. All they want to do is kill Taleban and it will be interesting how they deal with being contacted on the ground. Currently they seem rather blasé. They will happily leave the PB without helmet or body armour. They came with various weapon types – Ak-47s [assault rifles], M-16s [rifle] etc. as well as what looks like a couple of bags full of RPGs [rocket propelled grenades] – could be interesting.

We are heading out to compounds 24, 22 and 19 tomorrow am, where 7 Platoon were contacted from a week ago.

1 May
My first contact. At mid-morning the platoon moved

over the canal towards where they were contacted a week ago. We moved south as a platoon, manoeuvring different sections to always keep one foot on the ground.

As my lead section were moving S along an irrigation ditch they were contacted by accurate small arms fire. After a short burst, the gunmen whom we stumbled upon fled and with one other tried to flank my callsign. We moved to deny them the opportunity and moved E towards compounds 17 and 13. Once we had checked those we started to move back towards the platoon location.

I managed to push my lead section over the bridge but as I did so we came under accurate small arms fire from 4 or 5 firing points. I was pinned down and when a round splashed approximately 2 m away my heart was racing.

The radios were down and so I had no comms with either Silab or the gun line. I therefore had to use my own fire, a javelin, GMG [grenade machine gun] and sniper pair. Two javelin missiles were fired onto a firing point which eliminated one threat.

There were now just 7 bods plus myself stuck on the wrong side of the canal. We had to make the decision just to go for it. With a rapid fire from the platoon we sprinted down the bank, through the canal, back up the friendly bank and then tried to push back into the PB. More luck than anything else saw the platoon safely back behind sturdy walls, laughing at the contact we had just been in.

For me it is still the fear of making a wrong decision which sits heavily on my mind. I am responsible for every person within this PB and I fear that we will not always be as lucky as we were today.

At least today I proved to myself that I will not freeze the next time I get shot at. I do not expect this to be in the distant future.

2 May

Morale seems to go up and down very quickly here. This afternoon we got a delivery of mail. X has written again and I rather unexpectedly got a package from the d'Ambs which was very thoughtful. Pickled onion, monster munch, foie gras and a lovely cigar were top of the list.

We played *Deal or No Deal* which seemed to raise everybody's spirits, and tomorrow night is *The Army's Got Talent*.

However, lack of phone communication is a real dampener. Some of the guys have not been able to speak to their wives or children for three weeks now which is terrible. Although I am bottom of the list I would like to speak to mum, hopefully in the next few weeks.

3 May

Good news all around yesterday. The CLP arrived and not only a lot of post but also a generator. Although they had forgotten to fill it with oil, we managed to drain the snatch and use the oil from there to fill the generator. We also bodged a charger for the satellite phones and so hey presto, we now have power to the camp and a line to the outside world.

Got a parcel from dad consisting of a pot of tea, a bamboo cup, two batteries and a book of the cathedrals of England – random to the last item! Got a great parcel from X and a letter from X.

It has been fairly quiet here over the last two days. We were in a small contact two days ago that was over fast. Finding the firing points is the hardest part. Without that knowledge I cannot make decisions and am fairly useless. Paraang [a nearby base] has been hit hard and seem to be in contact most days.

Around the fort it is hard patrolling country. There is not much cover and therefore movement is restricted. If we move to the SW then extraction back is difficult. There is a canal directly outside which although gives good cover is terribly exposed on both banks and can be covered by at least three or four firing points. Although one must not set patterns, with only two routes into that area it is virtually impossible. There is a definite lack of steer from above as to how to play this one. I am yet to be given a definite mission and clarity as to my role out here.

7 May

Our first base attack last night. Paraang came under

attack at approx 10 p.m. with one firing point. They returned fire with 50 cal and small arms which from our sangars was an awesome display of tracer looping like fireflies out to the south and towards compound 17.

Just when we thought things were slowing down out to the west we came under contact with RPGs and small arms. The sangars responded very well with a powerful volley back to the firing points. At last we have been taken on our terms and although I do not think we managed to kill any enemy we would have definitely given them something to think about. Ferooz was again mentioned on the Icom as the main player instigating the attack. The signal strength was high showing his proximity to the fort. Two other names were mentioned which I recognise from our previous fire fights.

The most frustrating thing is that they take us on, on their terms. They are very accomplished at moving into firing positions using good cover and it is almost impossible to identify the firing points. I hope with time this will improve.

Spoke to mum this morning. I hope I have not scared her too much. Although I am sure that she appreciates or rather I think she must appreciate what I am doing out here. Don't think I should have mentioned the ambush a few days ago – it is hard as the two worlds are so far apart. I hope this journal will help to put things in perspective for those back home who want to read it. The best way of describing it is being on one long exercise with a complete lack of luxuries, and without the knowledge that in 5 days there will be a coach at the gate to take us back to the barracks and the luxuries of bath and bed.

The flies are uncontrollable. As I write this there are approximately ten crawling over my legs and an unknown amount swarming over my head. Amazingly once they have disappeared in the early evening they are replaced by another of life's annoying creatures, the mosquito. They seem to be able to infiltrate any clothing and get into mosquito nets like effective bank robbers. They then spend the next few hours eating their hearts out much to the annoyance of the body lying below.

But if life was easy then it would be easily boring.

†

Mark was fatally wounded by a single bullet in his shoulder during an early patrol and ambush two days later, on 9 May. He commanded his men back to safety and lost consciousness from bleeding within an hour. He never regained consciousness.

CHAPTER 6

FINDING OUT HOW
MARK DIED

We had switched off the machines at Selly Oak Hospital, but I knew little of what had happened in Afghanistan.

Sadly, I only very slowly found out how Mark had died, and so I had a long daily tussle with my imagination for many months. This painful process of finding out was somehow mirrored by the gradually increasing public awareness of the war in Helmand as more deaths occurred. The Defence Secretary had said in 2006 that he expected hardly a shot to be fired in this conflict and, until May 2009, fewer than 140 soldiers had died in the previous six years. Mark's death was an early one in that very difficult year; in 2009 there were more casualties than in other year of the campaign. This was now a war, soldiers there were being injured and dying, but there seemed to be relatively little public interest in the UK, almost a denial of it. The Prime Minister, Gordon Brown, appeared to have a personal distaste for the conflict. Iraq was a politician's embarrassment, a public wound not yet healed, and the country seemed not to be in the mood to embrace another battlefront. This public diffidence and a sense of not knowing were the background to Mark's death.

Days after Mark's death, David and I were told that Major General Bill Cubitt, head of the Household Division, would visit us at my home. I did not realise that it was an Army 'family' visit, and that perhaps he did not know any answers and just wanted to say he was sorry. But I missed the saying of it and saw instead what became a pattern: how hard it is to find the words to talk about these things. We sat in my sitting room with its tidy yellow familiarity, polite and strained. The setting up of the meeting, its formality, General Cubitt's presence and power, stopped me asking the difficult questions I wanted to ask. In the end I just asked why this young inexperienced officer on his first mission had been given such a difficult task, sent to such a dangerous area. He said Mark was very highly considered and extremely well trained. I knew that Mark had said that there were not enough soldiers to fight.

The first detail I knew about Mark's death was given in a letter from Lt Col Rupert Thorneloe, handed to me on 26 May 2009, two weeks after Mark's death and just before his funeral:

On behalf of the whole regiment and particularly his many Welsh Guards friends, may I offer you my deepest and most sincere condolences on the terrible news of Mark's death? I am painfully conscious that no words of mine can possibly compensate you for your appalling loss, but I wanted you to know that you are in all of our thoughts at this extremely distressing time. Mark was a hugely popular regimental figure and his tragic and untimely death has shaken us all.

Since his arrival in the battalion over a year ago, Mark has been commanding 7 Platoon in Number 3 Company. He made an immediate impression as a highly competent young officer – fit, professionally competent, and cool and decisive under pressure. He always demonstrated great concern for the welfare of his men and they in turn worshipped him and would have followed him anywhere. In short Mark impressed everyone here so much that he was soon rated as the best platoon commander in the Welsh Guards – against extremely stiff competition.

In Afghanistan Mark's platoon was attached to the Number 2 Company Group. 2 Company is responsible for securing the southern half of a district called Nad-e-Ali. Nad-e-Ali is a significant centre of most of the Helmand population situated just outside the provincial capital Lashkar Gah. The company has four patrol bases, one of which – Haji-Alem – houses Mark's platoon. Mark was the senior man in that small outpost – an enormous responsibility for a young platoon commander, but one which he was filling with his usual flair and seemingly effortless competence. Part of the routine in a patrol base such as Haji-Alem is to send out patrols into the surrounding area in order to deter insurgent activity and to provide security for the local population.

Mark was leading one of these patrols at 8.30 on 9 May 2009 when they came under a heavy weight of enemy fire. Mark took control of his part of the patrol, and extracted them to a position of care in a building. However a second part of the patrol remained pinned down by enemy fire. In order to gain the situational awareness necessary for him to make a plan to extract (from enemy fire) the other half of his patrol, Mark stood up in the doorway of the building that he was in. As he stood up he was hit in the shoulder by a single round.

When a commander becomes injured in a battle or in an exercise, particularly when the commander is as strong and effective as Mark was, things can often go wrong, but Mark's men reacted magnificently (probably because of the high standard of training that he had instilled in them). They rapidly gave Mark first aid, suppressed the enemy with a high rate of fire (killing two of them) and extracted the patrol back to the base, carrying Mark so that he could be evacuated by helicopter. Throughout this Mark remained conscious and with great calmness and presence of mind continued to tell his platoon what to do. I have no doubt that his actions that day will have saved lives. I understand that you have met Guardsman Gizzie, who was shot in both ankles as they made their way, under fire, out of the ambush site.

By the time Mark arrived at the hospital in Camp Bastion he had lost a great deal of blood and was critically ill. The medics did all they could to save Mark and commented on his exceptional fitness and fighting spirit which allowed Mark to make better progress initially than they had feared would be possible. It was possibly this that allowed them to Medevac Mark back to the UK and provide you with the very small consolation of being able to say goodbye.

I gather that arrangements are already under way for Mark's funeral and that it will be in the Guards' chapel. On the day of the funeral the padre here will visit all of our major patrol bases and conduct a memorial service in each one. We will also keep one minute's silence here in memory of Mark when the funeral begins in the UK. I know that you have already met Captain Darren Pridmore (the welfare officer in the battalion) and Colonel Tom Bonas (the Regimental Adjutant) but at this stage let me say that if there is absolutely anything that the regiment can do to help you or if there is any further information that you require then please do not hesitate to contact Darren, Tom, or me, at any time.

Mark's death was a tragic waste of a wonderful young life. Not only was he a truly outstanding soldier, he was also a thoughtful, charming and well-rounded young man. He had a wonderful sense of humour, and was an exceptionally popular and well respected member of the Officers' Mess. He was also held in deep affection by the soldiers he commanded. I have spoken to a number of them since, including Guardsman Gizzie and it is quite clear that they feel a very deep sense of bereavement at his loss.

May I once again offer you my deep condolences. I can only imagine the suffering that you must be feeling and I hope it may be some consolation if I assure you that your remarkable son will never be forgotten by his friends in the Welsh Guards. He was like a brother to many members of the Officers' Mess, and we like you will miss him terribly. In this difficult world the way that he lived his life was an inspiration to others and we are exceptionally proud of him and all that the stood for. I am very sorry.

Yours sincerely,

Rupert Thorneloe

This kind letter explained much, but even more importantly to me at the time, it gave me strength. Mark had kept going despite being injured and in pain. It was the least I could do to try hard, I was doing it for him – he would have wanted it. That thought fired me through much of the following years.

But to me the letter also felt a strangely limited account, leaving important questions unanswered. It did not explain what happened at the patrol base, when he lost consciousness, how he was taken back, how he was. I had seen Mark in Selly Oak Hospital, with his body working (albeit on life support) but the brain stem dead, unable to tell his body to breathe and perform its normal functions. All this had been carefully explained to me at the time. When had that happened? There seemed to be a silent gap.

For many months after this letter my imagination took what little facts I had and filled in the rest, often in frightening technicolour. Early morning nightmares about that day came without fail, shattering my sleepy waking and fostering my disbelief about it all. Mark's letters, the diary, emails and our short conversation had told me how it was, that dry dusty medieval place, and that was somehow embedded in my brain. I could see him being shot, sometimes with his blood soaked everywhere and sometimes losing blood slowly and painfully whilst the men around him were powerless, unable to do anything. Sometimes in this reliving he was in pain to the end, bleeding and limp; sometimes he had lost consciousness earlier and was carried back at peace. It was difficult, impossible, to control the power of these imaginings, their regularity and the sense of my impotence in the face of them. For me, my mourning and these fantasies were one: because of them I could not remember Mark as he was, as I had known him.

And then there was the day, somehow without meaning, a very private barren place. I was sad, crying inside much of the time. I knew I needed to find out what had happened, how Mark was, whether he was conscious or in pain, this mattered enormously to me. Perhaps part of me wanted to be as close as I could to him at that time, as I had always been. But, as any parent would, I simply wanted to know; he was my Mark, my son. At some level I understood that it would be very difficult for me to 'accept' his death, adjust to it, until I knew what had happened. Perhaps I thought that knowing would relieve or even take away these morning terrors: it might turn out that the facts were not as I thought. I so badly wanted to hear those clichéd words: 'He did not suffer'.

In June, a few weeks after the funeral, the Welsh Guards officers' mothers and wives were invited to a lunch at the Cavalry and Guards Club on Piccadilly, a very elegant place, its members' history displayed proudly on its walls. I saw a large painting of Captain Oates leaving the tent at the South Pole in a blizzard. Touchingly, our boys had arranged the lunch before they left. The mothers and wives there all shared a deep fear for their sons and husbands and, although they were strangers, they felt close. But I was the only person there who had lost someone and I felt somehow weighed down by the others' awareness – it had happened only to me and my son. I came home and, unusually, went to bed, low for the rest of the day. At the lunch another mother told me that she had heard Mark had had a heart attack on the helicopter. Was this the answer, I wondered? I was also told that Lt Col Rupert Thorneloe would come to see me towards the end of July when he was on

R & R (rest and recuperation) leave, to tell me exactly how Mark had been, what had happened. That felt a long time ahead; I would have to wait, but then I would know.

The Welsh Guards in London were trying to help and support me, and did so admirably, kindly and sensitively for many months and years. On 13 June I was asked to the Queen's Birthday Parade. It was a sunny day of pomp, pageantry and, in some ways, joy: the order and pride of the bands, the bravura of their music, the marching soldiers filled with courage and strengthened by the beat of the music and their mates all around. I remember feeling jealous: Mark could have been one of these men. Later that day, I saw Lt Col Thorneloe in a television linkup with Afghanistan in which he said confidently that they had all they needed and that the conflict was going well. But I heard much later that behind the scenes he had been outspoken to more senior Army officials in pointing out the hopelessness of the situation, the roads littered with IEDs, the shortage of men and equipment, and, finally, the day before Mark died, that men were stretched as far as they could be and that only limited operations should be attempted.

What I had seen that day was the grander public face of the Army, but what mattered was its contrast, the grime, pain and fear of war. Days after the broadcast, on 1 July 2009, Lt Col Thorneloe was killed by a roadside bomb whilst visiting the troops, 'leading from the front' in a poorly armoured vehicle. He was the third Welsh Guards officer to be killed within weeks – their leader – and it felt as if they were being ravaged.

But I knew little of the world of war and I was dealing with my own wounds, metaphorically licking them as only nature could tell me how to do. I felt I needed to know how Mark had been, how and why he had died, but I could not ask now, press the point. The Welsh Guards were fighting more battles under difficult circumstances and in June 2009 had begun a new offensive operation, Panther's Claw. This brigade-level operation was to clear the Babaji area of a large number of Taleban who threatened Lashkar Gah; if successful, they were to attempt reconstruction. It was to involve thousands of American troops and was to be an aggressive and intense operation, a man-heavy approach to a conflict that until then had been waged by single platoons in small patrol bases, asked to 'take the Taleban on single-handed', as one of the soldiers said.

Encouraged by the Welsh Guards in London, I wrote to the sergeant in charge of the platoon in Helmand to ask what had happened to Mark. He wrote back to me to say that he had not been at the PB at the time, but offering kind words, which touched me. I understood that these humane soldiers wanted to share, explain, help, make it better – they said nothing for fear of saying anything at all, it might be too much, they may breach the restrictions placed on information.

Finally, six weeks after Mark's death, I received a telephone call from Afghanistan from Lance Sergeant Leon Peek, Mark's second in command. Major Guy Stone, who had visited me by then, had suggested that he ring. The Welsh Guards had asked if I would like to visit Prince Charles's garden at Highgrove with a small party of Army wives, an invitation that as a gardener I could not resist. I was walking around those manicured arbours with their exotic hidden surprises when my mobile rang. There was Leon Peek, telling me through the crackly radio signal that he would prefer to meet me so that we could talk, so that 'we could cry together'. Those few minutes of contact with someone who understood meant so much, a tiny fragment of shared and somehow safe territory. He felt so close and all my sadness erupted. I can remember the salty tears running down my cheeks, uncontainable. This was talking to someone who would know how I felt, even who perhaps felt the same. I was grateful: it must have been a difficult call for him to make. But what he said implied a tragedy, something which had gone very wrong.

I knew that the Army had a policy of telling mothers and close family in detail about the deaths of loved ones, and that usually family were given the opportunity to talk to those who had been with them at the time. I had been told that Mark's Number 2 Company Commander, Major Bettinson, came home on R & R leave in July. I realised that his priority would of course be his family and, given the intensity of the tour, perhaps time alone.

But it was two months since Mark had died and all I had was that formal letter from Lt Col Thorneloe. I knew that, as Mark's commanding officer, Major Bettinson would most likely have been in direct radio contact with him throughout the ambush or been in charge in the ops room nearby. I hoped that he would telephone me or even visit, and I was very disappointed that I did not hear from him – with Mark's death so heavy in my head every day.

Then I received a letter from Number 2 Company Sergeant Major in Helmand, dated 31 July, saying that rather than tell me what had happened he 'would rather wait for the details and the facts to come out correctly as a result of the SIB's investigations [the Special Investigation Branch of the Military Police]'. Although it may have been well-meaning, this felt very hard for me at the time. I sensed a defensiveness there, more than the ordinary censorship I expected, a brigade operation which was not to be discussed with me. What had happened to my boy?

Following this, a senior Welsh Guards officer in the UK telephoned and said that the men remained upset, and that I should not be told more in case it interfered with the expected Coroner's inquest into Mark's death. We were not to be in contact if they came home on R & R. This was my son – I wanted to know what had happened to him and bowing to an administrative legal process felt wrong, shallow and very insensitive.

My initial anger over this finally dissolved into a heavy sadness, there all day every day, even more of a burden now with time and waiting.

At times I felt slightly like a child must feel being kept away from the funeral of a parent, ignored in the face of greater power. The Welsh Guards had been Mark's alter-family, they said that they were now my family also, so why could I not be told what had happened or even talk to the men? The fighting soldiers and officers I had met were straightforward, well-meaning people. What was getting in the way? Surely this was what the inquest was to be about: to get at the truth, not reinterpret it. I had been in touch with the Coroner's assistant in the weeks following Mark's death, so I checked with her that there was no legal issue here, and she said that from the Coroner's point of view this was fine.

I did not understand this caution, was it really because of the men's upset? I wondered if perhaps the Welsh Guards in Helmand were confused about what had happened in the heat of the battle, not sure what explanation there was to be had. They were still fighting and might hardly have had time to consider their sadness about Mark's death; that would come later when back from the tour. Some young Welsh Guards officers did visit as they trickled back on R & R, kindly telling what they knew, but they knew little: all platoons operated in distinct groups, albeit under a battalion banner. They tried to reach out, explaining what they could, the situation, the territory, but they did not know what had happened to Mark. I did not want to push them about it; Mark had been their friend, they too were very sad.

The Army padre came to see me and told me of his affection for Mark, how Mark's first words when they met were to ask him to a party, dog collar and all. He had been with Mark at Bastion Hospital that Saturday and had seen Mark there covered in blood after surgery when there seemed to be still hope. But when he saw him again on the Sunday, by now cleaned, hope seemed to have gone.

Steve, my support officer, could tell me little. The MOD welfare care was excellent, perhaps even excessive as so many people contacted me to help with the various different administrative tasks after Mark's death. But I wanted something other than that, information which it could not give.

Finally, on 20 July, more than three months after Mark's death, the MOD issued an 'initial account' of Mark's death, uncontroversial in its sterility and confusing in many ways.

After approximately thirty minutes of patrolling they reached the compound and came under fire from multiple directions. It was during this enemy contact that Lieutenant Evison was shot in his right shoulder. A member of the Fire Support Team carried Lieutenant Evison back to the Command Post, and whilst doing so he noted that Lieutenant Evison was losing a considerable amount of blood. Lieutenant Evison received initial emergency treatment, as well as being administered morphine, by the medical staff at Patrol Base Haji-Alem, however, he remained unresponsive. Treatment was continued en route to the Role 3 Enhanced (R3E) Hospital at Camp Bastion including chest seals being applied to both the entry and exit wounds.

On arrival at Camp Bastion, Lieutenant Evison was taken to the Role 3 Hospital and received emergency surgery to try and stop the bleeding that the projectile had caused. Twenty-four units of blood were used during this surgery. He was stabilised and admitted to the intensive care unit within the hospital. However, he continued to suffer from internal bleeding and was taken back for further surgery.

The decision was made to medically evacuate Lieutenant Evison back to the UK for further treatment. Prior to leaving Afghanistan a CT scan was conducted which revealed that Lieutenant Evison had damage to his brain and one of the doctors stated that his injuries were incompatible with survival and that this damage was as a result of him having been in cardiac arrest for a long period.

But the report did not say what had caused the brain stem death. Presumably 'his injuries' meant the brain damage since his body had been working, although on life support, but that was not made clear. I did not understand what 'remained unresponsive' meant – it implied being unconscious when he arrived at the patrol base, but I knew later that this was not true. I had managed to speak to the US helicopter pilot who flew Mark to Bastion Hospital, and he was clear that Mark needed resuscitation and was 'struggling' during the helicopter trip, but he had not gone into complete cardiac arrest even then.

Knowing that I too was struggling, although in a different way, a medical friend with good Army connections asked a doctor who had been involved at Bastion Hospital and was now back in the UK to contact me. Thus, in early August 2009, the anaesthetist who had been there with Mark rang me, and I was given the first details about how Mark had been when he arrived at the hospital, some inkling as to what had happened to cause his brain death. Having checked first with the Coroner, he gave me a brief medical outline. When Mark had got to Bastion Hospital soon after 10 a.m. on 9 May he had just gone into cardiac arrest, and the medical team spent ten minutes massaging the heart directly, managing to revive it. He said that the bullet had torn Mark's subclavian artery and that his survival depended on surgery to clamp the blood vessel. His condition finally would have depended on the extent of the blood loss and the length of time he had been in cardiac arrest. He said that following the battle Mark had been taken to the patrol base, and that a US helicopter was launched around 9.30 carrying guns but no blood or fluids for transfusion, and only a paramedic on board, no doctor. The helicopter arrived at the patrol base to airlift Mark at 9.47. From what the doctor said, he believed the time taken to pick up Mark by helicopter would have affected how long he had been in cardiac arrest, and so his final condition and chance of survival. He had not suffered from internal bleeding as a result of the injury.

I felt very reassured by this doctor's willingness to inform and give the detail he knew from the medical notes: this was good NHS practice, which I recognised. He chose to give me very precise details about helicopter times, and it was easy to read into this some covert dissatisfaction with the helicopter delay. From what he said, there appeared to be certain other issues, perhaps with the medical pack as Mark had suggested in his diary, perhaps with fluids. This sketchy outline was a real comfort at the time, though I still longed to know how Mark had been in himself, whether he was in pain, what he had said.

Only days before the anaesthetist rang, I had seen a report in *The Observer* on 26 July 2009 by Mark Townsend, 'Lack of helicopters puts injured troops at risk', saying senior Army surgeons had claimed that injured British troops in Afghanistan 'are enduring lengthy delays before receiving hospital treatment because of a shortage of helicopters' and that a dedicated fleet of medical helicopters had been requested from Whitehall as early as

2007. The MOD had publicly denied the risk to troops, saying that no soldier had died because of helicopter delay. Cynically, I wondered if reclassifying casualties in terms of 'X would have died anyhow' allowed the MOD to exclude those deaths from helicopter delay statistics. I had heard of such cases previous to Mark's.

Sadness, regret and uncertainty were a constant dominating part of how I felt inside, but there was the public to face as well. After the *Newsnight* interview and the publication of the diary, I was slowly catapulted into a world I knew nothing about, which I had not expected to enter. It was very different from the medical world that I knew. Journalists were interested in Mark's story and his diary, and later I was often asked for interviews, occasionally agreeing if I felt it served a useful purpose.

There were also occasions that were there to comfort. As Colonel of the Welsh Guards, Prince Charles invited Elizabeth and me to tea on 30 July at Clarence House – he invited the families of fallen soldiers in his regiments to meet him a number of times over the next two years. It was just ten weeks after Mark had died. For me, that day was one of my bad days, days when my feelings felt too close to the surface, slightly out of control, and which I came to dread. Would I break down or behave inappropriately in some way? We were ushered into a reception room on the ground floor of Clarence House, and then to a cosy upstairs suite, family photographs and memories all around. Prince Charles walked towards me, hand outstretched, the person I recognised from so many photographs, and, distracted and without thinking, I just said 'Hi.' That seemed to establish the mood of the meeting, and we stayed twice as long as the forty-five minutes planned. This thoughtful, charming and humane person was able to feel where we were, understand our grief and speak to us almost as if we were family: we were after all part of his Welsh Guards family. He was able to share those things that mattered to me – children, gardens, death and the human spirit – as we laughed and chatted about the minutiae of making wild gardens work, keeping sons off motorcycles and dealing with tragedy. He comforted with the lightest touch, and I could admire that at the time. I could sense in him that special understanding that those who have suffered in the same way can bring. I saw him speak so easily to other soldiers' families after this.

Gordon Brown had written to me after Mark's death, an undated letter, as he did to all the parents of dead soldiers. It was as follows:

Dear Mrs Evison,

I have been so sorry to hear of Mark's death in Afghanistan and I want to offer, from Sarah and me, our heartfelt and sincere condolences, and to assure you our thoughts are with you at this terrible time.

Mark was an outstanding young officer, serving his country with courage and pride, and highly regarded by all those who worked with him. The country owes him a huge debt of gratitude.

Please let me know if Sarah and I can be of any help.

With deepest sympathy,

Gordon Brown

10 DOWNING STREET
LONDON SW1A 2AA

THE PRIME MINISTER

Dear Mo Brown

I have been so sorry to hear of Mark's death in Afghanistan and I want to offer, from Sarah and me, our heartfelt and sincere condolences, and to assure you our thoughts are with you at this terrible time.

Mark was an outstanding young officer, serving his country with courage and pride, and highly regarded by all those who worked with him. The country owes him a huge debt of gratitude.

Please let me know if Sarah and I can be of any help.
With deepest sympathy,
Gordon Brown

I decided to write to thank him, and suggested that it would be helpful to speak to him, an invitation almost implied in his letter. In mid-July Harriet Harman, the local MP for Camberwell & Peckham, visited me at home to express her sadness about Mark's death, and during the conversation she asked me if I would like to talk to the Prime Minister. I mumbled a reply, by then hardly interested. Then an invitation came to speak to him at Downing Street on 17 September for half an hour. I was later told that he had seen other mothers of deceased soldiers.

It felt like an important meeting. I wanted to use it well, perhaps even try to make some difference, but at least to remind the Prime Minister of how it was out there for our soldiers. I thought about the meeting carefully beforehand, I did not want to waste his time, or indeed mine – how could I say anything useful to him? Intuitively I understood that it would not be helpful to be angry or confrontational with this man. To fall back on political policy would be all too easy, our discussion would have no impact, it would feel like home territory for him. I was aware that on a visit to Selly Oak Hospital some injured soldiers had refused to meet him because of the lack of support for the conflict by senior Labour Party politicians.

I walked through the barrier at Downing Street, an ordinary person off the street. I wanted to be just that. This man moved with generals, the senior Army, statesmen and politicians; I wanted to say something different. I was ushered in and walked up the wonderful yellow staircase lined with portraits of past prime ministers. I was shown into the main room, a long, elegant and cosy room divided into three areas, the end part decorated by Mrs Thatcher following the IRA bomb attack of the 1980s. I liked its understated homely quality, with great but somehow self-effacing paintings lining the walls – there was little grandeur here. I was seated on one of two comfortable sofas facing one another in the central space, and waited for Gordon Brown. He came in alone, walked towards me to shake my hand and immediately said how sorry he was, that he wanted to offer me any support he could.

Every time he talked politics I gently chided him and reminded him that I was not interested in that, politics was not what we should talk about. I wanted to tell him that Mark was a person, not just a faceless soldier. I took in the transcript of Mark's diary with its account of shortages and being 'on a tightrope', and explained what I had become aware of – how life was for ordinary soldiers on the front in this unexpectedly difficult theatre of war, how lack of men, equipment and even water were ordinary experiences. I told him about Mark's injury and death, as I had been able to establish the facts.

I discussed with him the moral dilemma that I could see was faced by those fighting: should the Army do its job and fight, or choose not to fight because politicians and senior civil servants had not made adequate services and equipment available? Soldiers and perhaps local commanders were aware of the problem but why not some of the very senior officers, the MOD, even the public? There seemed to be an issue across the defence establishment, those at the top apparently not knowing enough of what was happening at the bottom. I said that at the hospital where I work I had been impressed that the senior team managing the cancer unit was extremely aware of the services 'on the ground', every month monitoring and discussing individual cases of poor management. I knew that the NHS had turned itself around to be a user-friendly service by inviting comment, criticism and help in the planning of new services from those using them. It seemed to me that perhaps the Army establishment and the MOD needed to do the same.

I wanted the Prime Minister to understand that this was about a young man, a son and a friend, and so I took in a large beautiful book of photographs of Mark made up by his friends after his death. It is bound with a wide peaceful photograph of Mark fishing, and under the title, 'Lieutenant Mark Evison 1st Battalion Welsh Guards 17 July 1982–12 May 2009', is written, 'A hero is a man who is frightened to run away'; on the back cover, beneath another photograph of Mark, 'The hero is one who kindles a great light in the world, who sets up blazing torches in the dark streets for men to see by'. Inside the front cover is written, 'Mark Evison, our dearest and bravest friend. This book has been produced in loving memory of a true hero. Lt Mark Evison was killed in action whilst serving with the First Battalion Welsh Guards in Helmand province Afghanistan.' It is a wonderful touching statement by Mark's friends and it hinted at the effect of this death on them. I left the book with Gordon Brown, who said that he would show it to his wife Sarah.

The Prime Minister listened hard and appeared very interested, even keeping the Chancellor waiting for fifteen minutes. From how he was, I had to assume that he did not know about the things I was telling him. He seemed to me quite sensitive to those moral issues, a man who wanted to understand. I also knew he had lost a child himself with the unexpected early death of his first born. He offered to look into difficult aspects of Mark's death and, since no aide had been present, when I thanked him afterwards I reminded him of my queries about apparent helicopter delay, poor radio support, lack of air cover and medical equipment. He replied on 27 November, a three-page letter written by an adviser presumably close to the MOD, which sadly, but perhaps predictably, did not give any answers at all.

I had previously met Bill Rammel, then Minister for the Army, when he had appeared on *Newsnight* with me in July – at the time he had suggested that I should come to talk to him. On 14 October he invited me to the MOD offices, and during our conversation he said he was aware that Mark's soldiers had been cautioned against speaking to me because of the inquest. He said he was surprised and that this was not usual policy. My personal suspicions, which before had been a cloud of uncertainty, were now concrete with his statement. Why had it happened in Mark's case, I wondered; why was this unusual? Was there something to hide? Or was it the Army clamping down, closing ranks? Why had other mothers I knew been so closely informed, treated so differently?

The Welsh Guards returned around October that year. On 15 October Major Bettinson visited me with two other Army officers, but again it was easier to talk about the good times with Mark, and issues such as possible helicopter delay or what had happened were avoided or left unsaid. Some members of the platoon came in early December in a group, but they were accompanied by a junior officer, and again little was said about how Mark was when he died, what had happened.

From then, I slowly met other soldiers from the platoon, the arrangements made between us privately through a social networking site. Only on a one-to-one basis were they comfortable with giving me details. It is hard to describe how important this was for me and, I think, for them. I became aware of how much pain medication Mark had had (it seemed very little to me, but enough to help), how he had been conscious for such a long time, what he had said, and how he had found it difficult to see in the last hour, asking who was there. The facts were not dissimilar to my morning terrors, but they were facts and they were shared. The men told me how they tried to look after him, how much they had cared, and from their tears I could tell how upset they had been. We could talk and know there was nothing that we had to hold back, nothing that would shock because it was all shocking and we all understood. Some of the men appeared to have symptoms of post-traumatic stress following the incident, and from my work as a psychologist I knew it was a good thing for them to talk. It was a huge relief to us all, as we sat there crying together. They felt better, as did I. It felt almost like a chance to reconstruct Mark, to have him back a little rather than not at all.

Gdsm James was the first to ring me, several weeks after the soldiers had returned to the UK. He apologised to me for taking so long to telephone, but said that he had been too upset to do so. We talked for about an hour and both wept as he told me how he had been the first to give Mark medical attention immediately after he had been shot, how Mark had asked for morphine but because he was not sure that his lungs were clear, Gdsm James felt he should not give it and bravely refused him, saying, 'Sir, you will have to be a man.'

Gunner Steven Gadsby met me in a pub in Stevenage in December. He said he had not talked about it before, he could not talk to his parents and his girlfriend did not want to discuss it. Again, we cried and cried. He was with Mark for much of the time after he was shot and carried him part of the way back across the dangerous open infantry bridge into the PB and under fire, then returning to bring in Gdsm Gizzie. Later he was awarded the Conspicuous Gallantry Cross for his actions, and he asked me to join him and his girlfriend when he was given the award, first at Royal Artillery Armoury House and later at Buckingham Palace. We often talked after, as he seemed to want to try and help me deal with my burden.

I met Gdsm Joe Korasaya, a big strong Fijian who had carried Mark most of the way back to the patrol base. He said he could not sleep because of nightmares about the blood down his front; he would drink himself to bed. He had not discussed it with anyone; the only person he was close to was his mother in Fiji. He continued to text me at anniversaries.

I needed time after these meetings to absorb and adjust. I knew Mark was a brave person and could probably deal with pain, and I was gradually able to accept the facts. Two Army padres listened to my upset, helping me accept it as I talked it through. I was supported and helped by my GP, who explained medical matters: how even that small amount of morphine would have helped Mark relax and given some relief. I was told that Gdsm Gizzie had turned down morphine despite a bullet through both ankles and that gave me some comfort, hearing of a soldier who did not need morphine to deal with pain. Perhaps that had happened to Mark also – he had not needed it. Though difficult, this talking and sharing with Mark's soldiers was one of the most comforting parts of the journey. Their deep kindness and straightforwardness impressed me; they seemed matured and somehow centred by their experiences as soldiers.

What the soldiers said was supported by the SIB Military Police report, given to me by the MOD in December 2009 in preparation for the Coroner's inquest. Looking at this document always left me flat, sad, but I knew I had to read it for the inquest. It was a compendium of individual soldiers' accounts of that day – 9 May 2009 – when the men were back at Company HQ, several weeks after the event because of the difficulty of getting to the patrol base. There was relatively little difference of opinion amongst the men about what had happened, and it seemed strange to me that the MOD had nervously anticipated that any discrepancies would be too hard for me to reconcile. Some soldiers put in more details and some were in different places, but the story was consistent and hung together.

Slowly, the public interest in Afghanistan was increasing as each Helmand death was announced on television and bodies were repatriated to Wootton Bassett. There were 200 more young men lost in just over a year after Mark died, and the Queen kindly gave the loved ones of those fallen a national token, the Elizabeth Cross. This was presented to the families of the Welsh Guards by Prince Charles at Clarence House. The public distaste for these deaths was palpable. The Prime Minister fell at the general election, criticised for being heartless – his last words as he resigned were his thoughts for the soldiers and bereaved families. The incoming politicians pledged to support the war in Afghanistan, and to do what needed to be done.

Through talking to the soldiers in late 2009 and the delivery of the SIB report and its attached medical report that December, I was finally beginning to piece together what had happened. I had Mark's account of shortages and difficulties on the ground, and I had talked to the various soldiers about Mark and how it had been for them. I knew what had happened in Bastion Hospital. But there was still a gap: how had Mark become brain dead? There were still questions surrounding Mark's death that had not been answered. I did not understand what had happened with the helicopter; why the men and Mark were left waiting for such a long time. I was now aware of the MOD's defensiveness but unsure what to make of it. The Coroner's inquest was approaching – it would be the Coroner's job to explain, I thought.

Finally, nearly a year after Mark's death, in late April 2010, I was given a copy of head camera footage of Mark's death taken by one of the soldiers. These head cameras are sometimes used, against orders, to record what happens in the field, and footage is posted on YouTube for friends and family back home to see. The footage had been handed in to the SIB by the soldier's parents around July 2009 and then given to the MOD. I watched it alone in my kitchen, not wanting to upset my immediate family and friends. I watched, terrified of what I might see.

There was familiarity all around me in the kitchen but the screen invited me into another world. The headcam viewpoint was chaotic as the helmet weaved and ducked, the soldier wholly involved in dealing with the situation at hand. I could see the flat wide landscape, occasional small scrawny trees, the red mud roads baked hard, lined with the shallow muddy ditches, the blue sky above. I could see the high windowless walls of the occasional family compounds. There were no farmers to be seen, no one to make this a living landscape, the setting instead one of empty desolation. I could hear bursts of peppered shots, some more distant, and finally the scream, 'Man down.' This was my Mark.

Then they were back in the patrol base, a large space with its wide thick heat-baked walls, filled with wire and the paraphernalia of war. There was Mark, lying on the ground, a distant figure but unmistakably him. Others were looking to him, calling him urgently: 'Sir, sir, you're gonna be in the pub in a couple of days'; 'Sir, sir, keep talking, sir'; 'Sir, you're gonna be alright.' The men with panic in their voices as they waited for the helicopter, no sign of it yet, and then finally a weak and tired voice, 'I'm going down,' and again, 'I'm going down.'

CHAPTER 7

FIREFIGHT AT HAJI-ALEM

So what happened that day, the day described later by the soldiers as the worst of their time there, the day that changed some of their lives, the day some remembered as an emotional divide, 'life before' and 'life after'?

Machines, men and morale win wars – in April 2009 the situation those Welsh Guards found themselves in was not good. As Colour Sergeant D. P. Brown, an intelligence warrant officer, recorded in the SIB Military Police report, 'enemy fire have quickly understood these points and understand when troops are vulnerable'. This was a high risk operation led by a talented but newly trained lieutenant just twenty-six years old, supported only by junior non-commissioned officers and a much diminished platoon, down from twenty-eight men to twenty-two men. Most of the soldiers had not seen combat before, most were barely out of their teens.

The Nad-e-Ali district was a very dangerous part of Helmand, unsettled and unfriendly. With the poppy harvest completed, trouble was expected with a new influx of insurgents. From the time they arrived, all four patrol bases in the district (Haji-Alem, Tanda, Paraang and the Company HQ at Silab) were almost always under attack. A few kilometres away at Marjah was a Taleban training camp: the new Taleban recruits used these PBs for first practice, whilst the Allied forces were to act as a 'buffer' to prevent infiltration to the rest of Helmand. But the Taleban were hard to see, expertly hiding in compounds, amongst trees or along the putrid irrigation ditches lining the fields.

There were too few soldiers – enough to man two bases, but these had to be spread to four. The description from Lt Col Rupert Thorneloe's letter that their aim was 'to deter insurgent activity and to provide security for the local population' seemed unrealistic and idealistic even to me. On 8 May Lt Col Thorneloe told his seniors at brigade level that the Welsh Guards were not sufficiently resourced to provide more than limited battle group activity, that deterring the enemy was not possible at present because of the shortage of men and the difficulty of their position, and that reassuring the population and winning the locals over was pointless.

Of the four PBs, Haji-Alem was the furthest away from the HQ at Silab, about 4 km east and deep behind enemy lines. It was in a very poor position with limited mobility routes. If the soldiers left the base by the exit over the bridge they were easily seen and were shot at as they patrolled; if they stayed they were shot at in the PB. They felt compromised, the Taleban in control.

The PB was isolated despite being only a kilometre from a key road junction, Green 9. Because this junction was just out of their sight, the Taleban were able to seed it and the supply route liberally with IEDs to very good effect. Supplies could only come irregularly, taking many trucks, over 250 men and nearly two days to deliver. There were insufficient helicopters for delivery by air. Initially priorities had to be restricted to ammunition, water, rations and medical kit; the men had no letters from home to keep up their morale, no batteries for phone calls and contact with the world. Frequently there were shortages of water, and water rations became more and more strict until once they fought one battle with no water for seven hours. The battery shortage had been a major problem: they did not have chargers for the VHF radios and there were no satellite telephone chargers. Finally a generator arrived but without oil, so they siphoned this off from a vehicle abandoned nearby. Supply and procurement seems to have been very shoddy, and they often lacked simple spares for important equipment.

Radios were all-important. VHR or Bowman radios were carried by the senior soldiers on the patrol and had variable reception, subject to 'black holes' caused by certain geographical conditions such as the presence of foliage or trees. PRR (personal role radio, or inter-personal radios) often worked very poorly and had not been supplied to all the men.

The soldiers' lifeline in the fight against the Taleban was their ability to draw down air support, fire power to frighten them away. This was Lance Bombardier Andrew Spooner's job, with help from Gnr Gadsby, using their superior Harris 117 TacSat satellite radio to call for help from Apache helicopters, which would be in the air almost immediately. But this satellite radio was disabled, one simple part missing, an antenna, after the previous skirmish with the Taleban. The spare was very hard to come by and then had to be delivered by road, and a replacement was not sent for two weeks after first requested. The day of the ambush, LBdr Spooner felt 'useless', unable to do his job, unable to radio for air support.

A few days before Mark's death a civilian had been injured at Haji-Alem, the son of a local elder. The US Black Hawk medical helicopter arrived after about forty minutes, and Gdsm Jon Caswell said to Mark that he hoped it would be quicker if one of them were injured. Mark reassured him, saying that the Army would do its best to look after its own.

Until an interpreter arrived, the soldiers were limited in their patrols: the platoon was impotent, restless with unbearable heat and flies, fighting men not able to fight, contained in the patrol base or going on short patrols and still being attacked.

Mark referred to the lack of clarity about their role, what they were doing there. He and some of the men could see that to 'dominate' the area was unrealistic, even to be a presence was very difficult and to patrol danger-ous. They knew that the Estonian soldiers there before them had limited patrols to 50 m. A 'hearts and minds' relationship with the local people was not possible. They could see the farmers going to work and trying to make a living, sometimes the children, but after the harvest there was war everywhere – and the locals fled. At a patrol base the issue became survival, not the hearts and minds of the locals.

They played games to distract themselves, sometimes rough and extreme in this barren environment and clearly great fun. Mark as ever was cheerful, watching the men and supporting them, helping to them keep positive. He would take them casually into his corner, talk to them about home, remind them of another life. He understood that care and fun would make this more bearable, bind them as a team alone in this isolated place.

They were boys from home, often friends from the peaceful Welsh valleys, in it together, looking after one another rather than themselves. They had joined up for many reasons: to have a job, to patrol and carry a power-ful gun, to go to war, to see the world. It was often a frightening surprise when they first saw combat, when they realised the danger: as well as almost enjoying the fear, the 'combat high' and rush of fighting, some realised they were 'fragging' (fragmenting) their heads for 'later', a later often peppered with flashbacks and nightmares. Sadly, many left the Army after this tour.

The following is a description of what happened on the day of Mark's death, taken from accounts given by the soldiers as part of the SIB Military Police investigation.

Helicopters were provided by the Joint Helicopter Force (JHF) based in Bastion, 20–30 km and a helicopter operation of about 15 minutes away from the PB. The actual tasking of helicopters was complicated: it was done through the Liaison officer in the Brigade HQ 'chatroom' at Lashkah Gar, 12 km away from Bastion. This control room was the central hub for the doctors wanting information, the helicopter force, the whole operation. Requests for helicopters would go up from the Company HQ at PB Silab, where Major Bettinson was in charge, through to the WG Battle Group Ops Room at Bastion, and then up to the Brigade HQ at Lashkah Gah. An officer from the JHF had been to Haji-Alem before the platoon arrived and knew that it was too small for a large UK Chinook helicopter to land within it, and too dangerous and difficult for a Chinook to land outside it because of IEDs and the canal next to it. The Americans could help with medical helicopters and took a pride in getting their Pedros into the air in minutes.

A 'nine-liner', giving nine items of information, was a call for help, and would be assessed and dealt with up the chain of command. There were three levels of urgency, level A was fatal, level B was within two hours, and level C was for walking wounded and non-urgent.

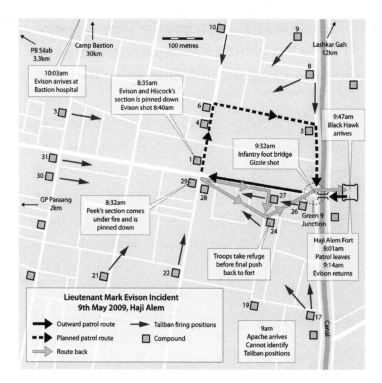

In his diary Mark had recorded shortages of radios and medical kit, and Gdsm Hobbs confirmed this: 'I did not have a Personal Role radio (PPR) and all commands I received were either by hand signal or other members of the patrol telling me.' Gdsm Austin also had 'no communication radio'.

Gdsm James, who attended Mark first as a medic, said:

I grabbed what medical kit I had. Which was a number of First Field Dressings (FFDs) a couple of CAT tourniquets [combat action tourniquet] and morphine. I did not have any HEMCON bandages [haemostatic dressings]

… The reason I did not have any HEMCON was because I had not been given my Team Medic Pouch, which I was given about 2 days later by Cpl Lacy at the PB.'

LCpl Lacy, the platoon medic, commented that when he went out on patrol he went with the usual ammunition and only a 'small medical pack'. This was for a three-hour patrol into very dangerous country and likely combat ahead.

Gdsm Lucas, in 1 Section and so left at the base that day, describes the area:

Haji-Alem is a small patrol base no more than 20 m square … The PB held about **[MOD deletion]** British soldiers all ranks and a further **[MOD deletion]** Afghan National Army. Lt Evison was the senior and only officer at the base. We had three junior non-commissioned officers (NCOs) plus attached personnel (1 sniper and two Javelin operators who formed the Fire Support Team). We had taken over the PB from the Estonians about 21 April 09. The PB has a tower on each corner and resembles a fort with a main gate facing west. The PB is surrounded by other compounds and many of these were used by enemy forces to fire Small Arms Fire (SAF), Rocket Propelled Grenades (RPGs) and PKMs (a faster fringe support weapon). We had very little to do with the local nationals in the area who could either come to the base for compensation claims or to tell us where they were working in the fields so we did not shoot at them – suspecting them to be enemy. The area was very volatile and when we went south east we were contacted every time [come under enemy fire].

Given the platoon's circumstances, the decision to go out that morning was a difficult one. Mark was in direct radio contact with the Company HQ, Captain Chris Lambe and Major Bettinson. Brigade policy was to try to 'dominate', to establish a fighting presence in the area, to show themselves as courageous and intrepid, and in the end be soldiers and fight – as well as, of course, to 'make do'. Mark had just arrived after a short illness, he had a job to do. But he was cautious about endangering his men, careful with his decisions. He was possibly not aware that the satellite radio was disabled. This tension between caution and attempts at dominance clearly needed judgement and policy, and that policy was not there at the time.

The patrol was initially briefed at 8 a.m. Their task was to investigate compounds to the north-west that the Taleban used as attack bases. They were operating under the NATO Rules of Engagement, protecting civilians. There were two routes they could take, with the one over the footbridge the more dangerous.

Gdsm Korosaya in 2 Section describes his experience after the initial briefing:

The aim was to go down a track using an irrigation ditch

and look into compounds 28, 29 and 1 to see if there were any civilians living in them ... there were known enemy positions in compounds 17, 19, 22 and 13 [due south, not on map] who were armed with small arms ... Throughout the patrol we would dominate the area in Haji-Alem to disrupt the enemy. If we received small arms fire we were to go firm and observe the enemy (if he acts suspiciously), suppress the enemy, call in mortars and guns and withdraw from the area ... The area was predominantly open ground with track with irrigation ditches on both sides and the area was surrounded by poppy fields ... We were operating under rules of engagement and ... the enemy threat was from IEDs and small arms fire with rocket propelled grenades. We expected to be on patrol a maximum of 3 hours.

Straight after the brief we deployed out on patrol in the area of Haji-Alem which is heavily populated by enemy forces ... To get to these compounds we followed a track in the south direction and crossed a bridge named INFANTRY BRIDGE which is in the direction of west. As we moved we call this pepper potting. One section holds the ground and gives covering fire whilst the other section moves.

LCpl Hiscock describes the area and the communication difficulties:

The ground we were crossing was flat open poppy fields

and wheat fields criss-crossed with irrigation ditches. The ditches are about waist high with knee-high water running through them. The compounds scattered around are made of baked mud and consist of an outer wall about 6 feet high and single story buildings inside … Communications in the area were difficult on the ground and back to 20 Silab were even worse … I can recall that during the contact we were having a lot of difficulty in getting communications with our HQ at PB Silab. Because of this we were unable to get direct fire support as we could not identify friendly forces locations … The enemy remained in good cover throughout the contact and it was very difficult to positively identify them and their firing positions.

Gdsm Evans comments on the purpose of the patrol:

[It was] to try and locate enemy force firing points suspected to be in compounds 28, 29, 1, 4 and 6 about 300 m west of the PB. We also intended to speak with any of the local nationals in this area, to gain information about the enemy forces in that area.

The platoon generally worked in three sections, each having a different task. That day two sections of the platoon were to go out, 2 Section and 3 Section. 1 Section stayed at the patrol base to provide fire as necessary. Mark was to attach himself to either of the sections on patrol, with his interpreter and two members the Fire Support Team.

They set off at 8.30 a.m. LCpl Hiscock's 2 Section left the PB first, followed by LSgt Leon Peek's 3 Section. Mark remained with 3 Section until they secured compound 28, and at this point attached himself to 2 Section, who were to move north to compound 1 some 50 m away across an intersection.

Gdsm Langley, with 3 Section, describes the sudden apparent enemy interest in the patrol whilst they were at compound 28 providing covering fire:

Whilst we were in compound 28 waiting for 2 Section to push through I saw civilians moving out of the fields going on a westerly direction. A man came out of compound 31, about 200 m to the west and stood in the middle of the road, he was staring straight down towards us and had his phone by his head. I believed he was 'dicking' us, i.e. … someone watching your movements and passing the information on to enemy forces so that they can ambush you. I told LSgt Peek about him and he agreed that it looked suspicious. He passed the information onto Lt Evison who authorised a warning shot … The man turned and left immediately. He was a FAM [fighting aged male], in his mid-twenties wearing a black dish dash and a black head dress. He had a short beard.

Gdsm Austin, also in 3 Section, describes the poppy

farming and the initial quiet, and then the realisation of this small number of soldiers that they were dealing with a planned ambush with many firing points and various targets, which quickly became a battle. At the same time, the PB was attacked and so could not give fire support.

At this time it was normal for LNs [local nationals] to be in the fields gathering poppies. About three minutes prior to being contacted by enemy forces, the interpreter in my multiple informed us that **[MOD deletion]** the enemy were saying to one another to make ready … If the interpreter says something is about to happen involving the enemy, most of the time it will. My call sign that had gone firm near compound 28 were the first members of my multiple to be contacted by enemy. The enemy contacted us from compounds 17, 19 and 22. At the same time CP Haji-Alem was contacted by the enemy from compound 13 A [not shown on map]. The reason that I am aware that the CP was under attack was that members of my sect had radioed to the CP for covering fire, however the CP had to refuse as they themselves were under attack. As soon as we were contacted from the compounds 17, 19 and 22 more enemy fire was received from compounds 29 and 30. I believe that compound 29 was engaging my sect while compound 30 was engaging the reset of the multiple at compound 1. Gdsm Edwards 27, Gdsm Gizzie and I began to put down suppressive fire down towards the enemy. Gdsm Edwards 27 engaged compound 29, Gdsm Gizzie engaged compound 19 while I engaged compound 22. [We] put down suppressive fire towards the enemy for about 30 minutes. I was not aware at this point that my multiple was being engaged from a 360 deg area.

Gdsm Korosaya, with 2 Section, describes the same moment:

We secured compound 27 and 3 Section were given covering fire by us to move to compound 28 … The atmospherics at this point I would describe as being abnormal … I could see farmers in the poppy fields moving out from the fields. This is a combat indicator that we were going to be contacted. Furthermore up until we arrived at compound 28 we had not been informed of any **[MOD deletion]**.

Whilst in compound 28 I could clearly see compound 1, our next objective, 50 m away … Lt Evison informed us on PRR that the enemy could see us and were making their weapons ready. Approx. 2–3 minutes later Lt Evison informed us again that the enemy would be shooting at us … At this exact time 3 Sect were contacted by enemy forces with small arms fire from the direction of the south. I could see rounds of ammunition landing by Guardsman Langley's right hand about 1 metre away from him … the rounds were coming from the west. Lt Evison told us that we had to extract to compound 1 … Everyone from 2

Section went into the compound. As we moved we were receiving small arms fire from the north.

Suddenly they were in a firefight. 3 Section was in an irrigation ditch beside compound 28, under fire; Mark and 2 Section were moving ahead. First they tried to retreat to compound 29 but there was too much fire, and so they took refuge in compound 1. They had been ambushed by a large number of Taleban fighters close by, perhaps 50 m away with about fifteen firing points, and now had virtually no communication and as yet no helicopter support.

Gdsm Korosaya describes Mark's difficulties with the radio system, how he moved forward to get a better signal to importantly call in air fire support from Silab, to speak to LSgt Peek. He was also trying to see where the firing was coming from to assess the situation visually:

I would describe the compound [1] as being about 60 x 40 m surrounded by a perimeter mud wall about 9 ft high ... Directly opposite the entrance on the east wall is another entrance gap to the compound on the west wall ... [both] approx. 3 m wide ... these are the only entrance into the compound ... We were being contacted by small arms automatic bursts of fire from 360 degrees.

I could see that Lt Evison was about 2 m from the [eastern] entrance to the compound with the interpreter stood behind him with a gap of about 3 m between them

… I knew he was struggling to get communications using his radio with 3 Section … I think he positioned himself closer to the gap in the wall [entrance] to get a better signal. He was looking out of the entrance towards the direction of 3 Sect which was south. I could see him speaking over his Bowman radio.

LCpl Evans, 2 Section, near Mark in compound 1, saw him also:

Lt Evison was attempting to use his Bowman radio to request fire support from the Company Command in PB Silab but he could not get comms on the radio from inside the compound, so he moved towards the door way of the compound out of the room he was originally in. This door exposed him to some fields in the east, which at this time we had not received any contact from that direction. When I saw that Lt Evison was exposed to the door way to the east I shouted, 'Sir, push into the compound.' He then pushed back into the room, but still could not get any comms so he went outside of the room again, he was then 3 or 4 m away from me, facing into the compound with his front exposed to the opening in the door.

Mark must have feared for the lives of all. How to deal with this? They were all young, frightened, inexperienced and very alone in this strange place.

Gdsm Tucker, also near to Mark then in 2 Section, could see that they could not easily get back to the PB:

I then was still in compound 1 … as by this point the enemy forces had outflanked my patrol from both east and west, they were now in the fields in between our location and the CP [PB], cutting my patrol off from returning to the CP.

LCpl Evans continues:

I then heard a burst of about 5–6 rounds come from the east and into the compound to where Lt Evison was stood. I looked at him and he was holding his left hand up, saying, 'I've been shot' … I could see something on the hand he was holding, which looked like blood. At this point I thought he had been shot in his left hand. I then shouted, 'Get into the fucking room.' I then saw him step back into the room just behind him. He then went out of my sight and all I could see was his feet on the floor … he was sat on the floor. I then shouted for Gdsm James, as he was the Team Medic in my section. I had shouted for the medic over PRR but because we were getting contact from the east, west and south the medic was cut off to cross the road to compound 1 due to fire power.

Gdsm Korosaya describes the shooting:

At the same time I could see rounds falling on the floor through the entrance landing about 1 m to the left side of his feet. The interpreter ran first away from the entrance towards the room … Lt Evison turned and followed the interpreter …

I could see a round of ammunition hit his chest on the right side between his body armour and the pit of his arm … I immediately heard the interpreter shout, 'Man down, man down' … Pte Gadsby was inside the room and came out and I could see him drag Lt Evison into the room … I saw the interpreter take off his body armour and helmet … At the same time the interpreter was calling for a medic. Gdsm James went straight into the room as soon as Lt Evison was shot. Gdsm James is a team medic also. After 2–3 minutes 3 Section and 2 Section gave covering fire for the medic to the south east to run to our location.

Gdsm James in compound 1 describes helping Mark initially:

I then ran into the room Lt Evison was in … [He] lay on the floor … he had his Osprey on and … had a wound to his right shoulder and there was a lot of … blood coming from his wound onto his Osprey … The ITT [interpreter] was also in the room. Lt Evison was also conscious at the time, he was saying, 'Make sure LSgt Peek has taken over charge.' I then took his Osprey off … At the same time I told Lt Evison that everything was OK and that he should concentrate on me, in an effort to keep him conscious. Gdsm Tucker was also in the room now. I then ripped his UBACS [under body armour combat shirt] off to see the wound. Then using his top I wiped the blood away from his wound where I could see the blood coming from a hole in his right shoulder, which was about the size of a 50p piece. I then got an FFD out and applied it to Lt Evison's chest and held it down to try to stop the bleeding as much as possible ... I was then getting Gdsm Tucker to radio for the RAMC [Royal Army Medical Corps] medic Cpl Lacy to come ... He was with LSgt Peek's section on the other side of the road to myself by compound 29 and due to the contact he could not cross the road. I then started to get slightly overwhelmed by what was going on and was very upset. I then checked Lt Evison's pulse which was quite slow. The FFD on his wound had now filled up with blood and I removed it and placed another on the wound. At this point Lt Evison was in and out of consciousness to the point where I shook him to wake him up. I checked his pulse again and it was getting slower. I can't remember how slow. But I immediately using my fist did what is called a chest punch to the area of his chest where his heart is, in an attempt to keep his heart beating ... It seemed to work as he woke up and stayed awake. Lt Evison then asked if I could give him morphine. I refused to give him morphine as where his wound was I did not know how much damage had been done to his lungs and because he was in and out of consciousness I did not want to cause any further problems, for example to his respiratory rate, which at the time was OK. I then continued to hold the FFD over his wound and keep Lt Evison talking until Cpl Lacy arrived about 5 minutes later. I believe that there was nothing I could have done without HEMCON or Quickclot. Cpl Lacy then arrived ... He then asked me if I had seen an exit wound, which I had not, so we then 'log-rolled' him over and I looked at this back where I could see a lot of blood but I could not see an exit wound ... We rolled him back over and Lt Evison said, 'Is there an exit wound?' I replied, 'I can't see one.' Lt Evison said, 'Well that might be a good thing.' Cpl Lacy then tried to put a HEMCON bandage into the wound but the bandage was too big, so I cut it up into four pieces and held the wound apart while he placed the HEMCON into the wound. We used all four pieces of HEMCON, with using pressure on the FFD and applying the HEMCON pieces the bleeding was starting to stop or at least slow down. I then applied a fresh FFD to the wound over the HEMCON and wrapped it around his body. Cpl Lacy and I then placed Lt Evison onto the stretcher...

Gdsm James found this very upsetting, and later wrote:

I did not see Lt Evison [back at the PB] as I knew there were enough people treating him and as previously stated

I was slightly overwhelmed by what had happened to him, therefore I did not want to see him again.

Gdsm Langley, in 3 Section near compound 29 over the road junction, describes their experience:

> We then started to get rounds coming in from the NE. I think they were very close to us, maybe only 50 m away … The cracks and thumps were very close and it was accurate so they must have been close to us without standing up … I stood up in an attempt to identify the enemy firing pints and ensure I was not shooting our own forces … While we were laying down suppressing fire I heard a scream from compound 1. We were getting rounds coming from the south, west and north. Every time one of us stood up I thought we would get hit. The PRR had gone down.

Gdsm Langley also writes how LCpl Lacy and Gdsm Richards, then with 3 Section, finally ran through fire to get to Mark with medical support and a stretcher, and how the situation was deteriorating:

> I saw Cpl Evans's head appear at the top of the southern wall of compound 1 and he shouted, 'Man down' … He replied it was a shot in the wrist and then shortly after wrist and chest. LSgt Peek went to the southern side of compound 28 to try and get better comms … Lacy jumped out and started to move across the open ground when a

couple of stoppages occurred stopping us from firing. Lacy continued to run down the track by compound 1 with bullets hitting the wall and ground around him. [Peek] had comms with 0 via Bowman. I could not hear what was being said but thought there was some sort of argument as he was swearing. LSgt Peek then said over the PPR, 'Boys, we've got one casualty, got no fast air, no helicopters, no MASTIFFS [Army patrol vehicle] and no guns. We're in the shit and we have to get out of here on our own' ... LSgt Peek then asked for a stretcher and Gibbon had one on him. Gibbon said, 'Fuck it, I'm going,' and we gave rapid fire as he got up to move across the open ground when a couple of stoppages occurred stopping us from firing ... Once there were stoppages and he went the last few metres with only fire coming from Spooner's rifle.

Mark's injury was reported as a level C injury when the first nine-liner was sent up because of the blood on his hand: this was changed within minutes.

The communication between the Fire Support Team and the air support helicopter had to be via HQ at Silab which was very cumbersome. Finally LBdr Spooner in 3 Section said (as he told me later) that he and LSgt Peek agreed to give it up and just run for it.

Gdsm Edwards writes about this lack of air support:

I then recall LSgt Peek who was 20 ft away from me on the Coy communications radio requesting artillery and attack helicopters. I could tell from what he was saying that he was not getting any joy from the asset he had requested. A couple of minutes later I heard and saw an Apache Attack Helicopter above me. The enemy forces continued to fire, the helicopter did not deter them at all. The Apache did not engage the enemy forces at all … I was told after the incident it was because they could not positively identify the enemy fire points.

Gdsm Austin also explains this:

Four … went to compound 1 and carried Lt Evison from compound 1 across the Main supply route in the area of compounds 24 and 26. The remainder of my sect gave covering fire so that they could move back toward CP Haji-Alem … LSgt Peek requested fire support in order to suppress or kill the enemy. It was at this point that I was aware that an Apache Attack Helicopter [AH] was in the area. The Fire Support Team lost communications during the contact as the antenna of their radio was broken. Normally the FST would direct the AH onto the enemy positions … The AH helicopter … requested that we put down green smoke in the general area of the enemy to identify their positions. We did not have any smoke left as we had used this up to cover our movements towards the CP. Without the smoke we were unable to identify the enemy to the AH…

Back in compound 1, Gdsm Korosaya helped carry Mark on a stretcher through the ditches to compound 28, then 24 and 26, on the way back to the PB:

I heard the commands for a stretcher over PPR ... Pte Gadsby and myself lifted Lt Evison onto the stretcher that was at the entrance ... Lt Evison was conscious, he was awake and talking he asked me for a cigarette and I lit a cigarette and put it into his mouth ... Lt Evison was laid flat on the stretcher and he was smoking as he was being carried and was speaking. Lt Evison told us that we had to get him out of there soon ... We ran out of the compound towards compound 28 as 3 section gave us covering fire. We left the compound and followed the track down and Lt Evison was carried by six of us. When we got to 3 Sect after travelling for approx. 50 m ... LSgt Peek said we had to carry Lt Evison out of the area through the irrigation ditch. We were still under small arms enemy fire the whole time and the irrigation ditch gave us good cover. I do not know what was going on with the rest of the section although I could hear LSgt Peek saying over the PRR, 'We are on our own, we have no support from mortars or guns!' The whole time we carried Lt Evison he was conscious and talking. We were also constantly talking to him also, I recall seeing white cotton inside his wound, this was not a first field dressing and there was blood coming through his wound through the cotton … We moved back to compound 28 where the irrigation ditch was knee high.

Gdsm Korosaya and the three soldiers found carrying Mark on the stretcher too cumbersome, slipping and sliding in the ditches, Mark rolling on what was almost just a sheet, which filled up, heavy with water. So Gdsm Korosaya offered to carry him over his shoulders through the water. He then carried Mark about 200 m through the ditches under fire, almost to the PB, stopping close by in compound 26. It was a huge weight with his own kit, and he was exhausted, almost too tired to get back himself.

Rather than carry him on the stretcher … as we could not fit through … I carried him over my shoulders … on top of my ECM pack holding onto his arms and legs. I was running … We did not stop at any time. During this we were under small arms fire. I took about 10 minutes to get back to PB Haji-Alem. Before INFANTRY BRIDGE I had to stop inside compound 26 because I could not walk any more due to the weight and I could not move my legs any more. As I carried Lt Evison he asked me, 'Who is this?'

Gdsm Hobbs recorded:

Upon reaching the area around compound 24 we stopped

and Cpl Lacy gave Lt Evison an injection of morphine at his request … administered in the top right hand leg.

Gdsm Korosaya continues:

Inside the compound Lt Evison was placed onto Gnr Gadsby's shoulders to carry. Lt Evison was still conscious. Gnr Gadsby carried Lt Evison the last 20 m across INFANTRY BRIDGE. At INFANTRY BRIDGE a stretcher had been placed on the ground. Lt Evison was laid onto the stretcher and LCpl Crombie from 1 Sect was waiting. Pte Gadsby and another two who I cannot recall, I think Gdsm Caswell carried the stretcher for approx. 30 m into PB Haji-Alem. I ran into the canal the bridge went over to give covering fire…

Gnr Gadsby thus ran across the bridge into the PB in the open rather than through the water as it was faster. He wrote:

So I then put him over my shoulder and ran with him to the PB Haji-Alem. I was still under heavy contact at this point. Lt Evison was still conscious saying he couldn't see anything. I could not see any injuries to his eyes. He was asking if his bleeding had stopped. As far as I am aware his bleeding had stopped.

They had brought Mark back in about thirty-five

minutes, under fire. They all worked together without their leader, and risked their own lives to do so. LSgt Peek had had to take over, to make difficult and important leadership decisions which he had not expected to make.

Gdsm Roberts, 1 Section and a runner between sangars at the PB, commented that as Mark was brought in to the PB 'he was conscious and shouting with pain, he was not speaking any words just noises … We ran into the PB and placed Lt Evison next to the stretcher we had placed on the floor in the medical area.'

Gdsm Caswell, 1 Section, had been at the PB throughout the contact:

When I saw Lt Evison he was conscious … I could see the gunshot wound was to his right shoulder, which had FDD applied, which was soaked in blood and therefore his wound was still bleeding. He said to me, 'Who's that?' I replied, 'It's Caswell.' He said, 'What's going on with this bleeding?' I replied, 'I'm going to stop it now, Sir.' From the way he was being I believed he had received morphine. Cpl Lacy then arrived into the PB … I then placed a fresh FFD to the wound and held a saline bag up for Cpl Lacy to then apply intravenous access to his left leg, through his leg bone, which at that point Lt Evison sat up and said, 'Fuck me, that hurt, what was that?' He then lay back down.

I remember hearing that radio communications were

really bad when the PB were trying to find out where the Medical Emergency Response Team (MERT) were.

Cpl Lacy and I found an exit wound on his back about 6 ins below where the entry had been on the front. We secured the already placed FFD around him and applied another to his exit wound. Lt Evison was still conscious and speaking, with his vision going. I grabbed his hand and he squeezed slightly which felt quite idol [sic] in a way that he did not have the energy to squeeze very hard … We had then received information that the MERT was close in, so we moved Lt Evison into a room within the compound to shield him from when the helicopter landed … I then went to treat Gdsm Gizzie.

LCpl Lacy was with Mark in the PB and confirms:

The bleeding had stopped in both wounds. I attempted to get an IV drip into his arm but was unable to. I then put an intaceos IV into his left tibia bone which is a quick way of getting IV into the system … We then moved the casualty into one of the rooms of the PB … and confirmed that the bleeding had stopped in both wounds.

LCpl Lacy in fact later told me that up until they moved Mark into the side room, minutes before the helicopter landed, he was still able to joke with his men, about them not being allowed to take his sister out on a date.

Gdsm Korosaya describes the tension in the PB as they waited for the helicopter:

Once inside the PB I could see people treating Lt Evison. I put my ECM down and ran over to the stretcher. Cpl 'Ben' treated Lt Evison. I think he put a needle into his left lower leg. Lt Evison was conscious and talking ... I knew a 9 liner report had been sent and when we arrived in the PB we were waiting for a CASEVAC helicopter. After 20 mins Cpl Spooner told us there was another IASF casualty in another place and we had to wait for another helicopter. The whole time I gave Lt Evison water by pouring it into a bottle top and into his mouth whilst we waited for the helicopter. He was conscious and talking the whole time until 5 mins before the helicopter arrived. He said to me, 'I am going down, I am going down.'

Gdsm Caswell then returned to Lt Evison. He was complaining that he was having difficulty in breathing and drifting in and out of consciousness. I think he then fell unconscious. Gdsm Austin then administered air by using a Bag Valve Mask (BVM). Cpl Lacy then felt for a pulse, there was no pulse or only feint [sic]. Cpl Lacy then carried out chest compressions (CPR) whilst Gdsm Austin continued with the BVM. Lt Evison then opened his eyes, the chest compressions were then stopped but Gdsm Austin continued further with the BVM. We received information that the helicopter was in bound, so I continued to reassure Lt Evison until the helicopter arrived. About 2 minutes later the helicopter arrived and Lt Evison was covered by a blanket ... We quickly ran him on and passed him over to the crew on board. Lt Evison's eyes rolled to the back of his head as we left the room he was in before we put him on the helicopter.

Gdsm Austin tells how he got back to the PB and went to help with Mark:

I moved into the CP ... The team after mine also came in ... I proceeded to Lt Evison ... I recall there was a FFD on Lt Evison's chest ... I am aware that Gdsm James applied a HEMCON to Lt Evison at compound 1. This did not work and was removed as the priority was to get Lt Evison back to the CP as we were under heavy contact. I applied pressure to the FFD on Lt Evison in order to stem the bleeding. Eventually Gdsm Korosaya took over applying the pressure as my arms became exhausted. On three occasions we lost Lt Evison ... his pulse or breathing stopped. On one occasion there was no pulse so the medic put a vent on Lt Evison's face while I performed Cardio-pulmonary Resuscitation (CPR) ... On another occasion the bag vent was taken off and Lt Evison stopped breathing and had no pulse. I gave mouth to mouth whilst Cpl Lacy performed CPR. The Medical Emergency Response Team took about 50 minutes to get to CP Haji-Alem to extract Lt Evison back to Bastion. Eventually the MERT arrived and took Lt Evison away.

Gdsm Tucker was also with Mark:

He also applied a drip to his leg which must have hurt him as Lt Evison jumped up saying, 'Who did that?' ... I stayed with Lt Evison still trying to stop the bleeding. Cpl Lacy was applying hard pressure to the wound. I kept talking to Lt Evison, at this point I could tell he was starting to slip into unconsciousness, by answering questions with one word answers. He was clearly losing colour in his face, going into what I would recognise to be shock. Lt Evison started saying, 'I am going, I am going' ... Constantly we were shouting to LBdr Spooner asking him when was the helicopter coming. He answered saying that they had sent a helicopter back to send another one and that they were going to be 5 minutes 15 minutes ago. Cpl Lacey then requested an oxygen mask from Gnr Gadsby. Lt Evison then fell into unconsciousness and Cpl Lacy then performed CPR. About 5 minutes later the helicopter landed in the CP, Cpl Lacey had to stop performing CPR for Lt Evison to be taken onto the aircraft. Gnr Gadsby, Cpl Lacy, Gdsm Korosaya and I carried Lt Evison onto the helicopter.

The rest of the men had to get themselves to the PB,

under fire all the time. They finally all got back, although Gdsm Gizzie in 3 Section was injured with bullets through both ankles as he tried to return. He writes:

I carried on returning fire while Lt Evison was taken in. We were then peeling in ourselves, returning to PB HAM …We were ordered that LSgt Peek would throw a smoke grenade to provide us with some cover as we could not use the bridge because it was too exposed. We had to run over the road, into the canal and out over the other side … we had to do this two men at a time … LSgt Peek threw another smoke grenade to give us cover. I picked up Lt Evison's day sack and we both ran together towards PB HAM which was about 70 m away … We both jumped into the canal and crossed it. The canal had water in it which was about chest high. I was weighted down with the LMG and Lt Evison's day sack as well as the ECM, so it made me slower than Gdsm Tucker. As I started to climb up the bank I felt an immense pain in my right ankle and then heard the crack of a bullet passing me at speed. I tried to get back up again but couldn't. I took the ECM off and Lt Evison's day sack and put them to the side to give me a bit of cover. As I did so I shouted, 'Man down!' … Moments later two people Gdm Langley and another came to my location with two ANA members and the interpreter … We all moved towards Cpl Crosby and he asked if I was okay to hop in. I said I could, then with the help of Gdsm Langley and the other FAC guy who was big, managed to get back up the bank and as quick as I could, hopped back with them to PB HAM, getting cover from Cpl Cromby.

Gdsm James notes that 'during the helicopter landing we were receiving heavy contact from enemy forces outside the PB' and Gdsm Lucas writes:

> The helicopter to casualty evacuate the injured took more than 40–45 mins to arrive. There is only room for a Blackhawk or similar to land in the PB. Anything bigger – like the MERT (Medical Emergency Resuscitation Team) in a Chinook – would have to land outside the PB and risk being shot at.

The wait at the PB must have felt endless – after all their efforts to get Mark and themselves to the PB he was now effectively dying in their arms. Their distress can be heard palpably on the head camera footage.

The end of this for the men was watching as Mark was helicoptered out and the dust literally settled. For three days they knew nothing, but assumed he was in hospital in England and so treated and fine. Finally, a girlfriend told one of them that she had heard that the recently arrived soldier at Selly Oak Hospital had died. Only then did they know.

Gdsm Austin describes the aftermath:

A few days after the incident Lt Evison died from his injuries. Members of my unit and I at CP Haji-Alem were not notified of this at the time. I am aware that some members of my unit found out about his death from the Facebook website. I think we should have been informed by our hierarchy and should not have received this information second-hand.

Gdsm Lucas writes:

I was informed about 2 or 3 days after Lt Evison returned to the UK for further medical treatment that he had died. This was through one of the guys being told by his girl-friend and then confirmed by Capt Lamb who had come to the PB as platoon commander to replace Lt Evison.

This was the death of their officer, not unlike a parent in his role, a close comrade as well as their friend. Had the Army just been thoughtless and, as in times gone past, not told its soldiers what had happened because they thought that would help? Had they forgotten to tell them? Did they not know? Or had they chosen not to give an account until the inquest? LCpl Lacy said he did not know the details of what had happened to Mark until at the inquest.

Within a short period of time at least two of the men were diagnosed with post-traumatic stress disorder, one of them blaming himself for many months afterwards for his part until he saw a replay of the headcam footage and realised how well they had pulled together, how they had done it all right at the time.

When they heard that Mark had died their anguish was silent and powerful. They worked together to make a memorial to him. Then they took to the Taleban, shooting in revenge.

YouTube later showed a short film backed by tough music, made by the men about their time in Afghanistan, with all its hot dustiness and fighting. It is very touching, fading out at the end to silence and showing the memorial they built from stones and Afghan bricks, pink tablets of baked mud and hair, a large rough Christian cross with a sign on it, 'The boss', and poems to Mark written on a board by the men. The film also shows the memorial built to their friend from the Welsh valleys, Toby Fasfous. This part of the film is a silent tribute to two friends through many strange times, Mark and Toby. The film ends, 'Gone but not forgotten. See you on the other side boys.'

Early in the summer of 2010 Mark's memorial was delivered to me at home, Afghan bricks in ammo tins, the large rough-hewn cross with 'The Welsh Guards' tattooed on it with a sharp needle, the nylon Welsh Guards flag, the boards. For many months it sat on my back terrace, facing the lawn and garden that Mark loved, a strange contrast.

Finally, after Mark's death the patrol base was abandoned because of its vulnerable position.

CHAPTER 8

THE CORONER'S INQUEST

The Coroner's inquest was one of the most difficult consequences of Mark's death. It felt like a heartless legal nightmare in the middle of another crushing nightmare.

At the time I thought that three major issues probably contributed to Mark's death: helicopter delay, radio inadequacies and poor infield medical support, all important issues for soldiers. Individual mistakes and irregularities were, of course, the stuff of battle and confusion, and not culpable or accountable in law or in any other way. But there were clearly other problems, rooted in decisions made from the padded chairs of Whitehall.

From the platoon's point of view, the helicopter delay was the principal issue that needed addressing. Those soldiers had risked their lives to bring Mark back to the patrol base; their choices about what to do were predicated on the belief that the higher levels of helicopter command would not let them down. They sat with Mark as he struggled to keep conscious, telling him that the helicopter would soon be there. There had even been an altercation, fuelled by the tension of waiting and Mark dying in front of them. Many of them suffered for years after, often rewinding the pain of that day. That delay needed explanation, for me and for them.

Initially, when I heard about the impending inquest, I knew very little about what such a hearing would involve. I assumed that the Coroner was there to help the family find out what had happened, that it was a broader fact-finding inquiry. There had been early clouds: I was contacted by a father still angry with the MOD and arguing with their lawyers through the courts about whether his son would have died anyway despite helicopter delay. Nevertheless, I began like most with a naïve belief that the law was the highest institution in the state and that none are above it, and I was trusting and optimistic that the inquest would help, make things better in some way.

But I was worried, worried that I would not cope with what I might hear in court. I often thought of not going through with it, walking away. At the same time I wanted to face the reality of what had happened to my baby. Did I want to know or not know, I asked myself frequently. What might be said in court that I found difficult to hear? I was still mourning and could cry easily, I had wept in private with the soldiers, but in a public court? In the end I decided I owed it to Mark, to Mark's soldiers, to myself and to others to be there, to help put it behind us.

I wanted to prepare myself. The first pre-hearing with the Coroner in Birmingham was cancelled in September 2009 because the SIB Military Police report was not yet available, so instead I arranged with the Coroner to go and see him in a room at his court to discuss the process. It was a strange visit in many ways. I was expecting a private and informal meeting, but to my surprise a number of MOD officials were present in the waiting area. A very senior Air Force officer introduced himself to me, saying that he was there dealing with another case but he would be helping to co-ordinate and manage Mark's case. Whilst I was with the Coroner, my ex-husband's 'support' officer came in unannounced. It was unsettling, too intrusive, another cloud.

At that meeting the Coroner carefully explained to me that his task was to detail how, when and where Mark was killed. Then, which came over rather oddly at the time, he was at pains to tell me that if someone would have died anyhow the circumstances did not bear further consideration at an inquest, and he gave a detailed example. There was almost an implication that this might be the case with Mark. But since the SIB Military Police report was not yet available, I knew he could only have had access to the one-page MOD initial account, which simply described Mark's condition in hospital the day after his injury:

Prior to leaving Afghanistan a CT scan was conducted which revealed that Lt Evison had damage to his brain and one of the doctors stated that his injuries were incompatible with survival and that the damage was as a result of him having been in cardiac arrest for a long period.

How could this document, which did not narrate the circumstances of Mark's injury, influence his thinking? It did not allow for consideration of any contributing factors at all.

Nervous about the experience ahead, I decided to try and get legal representation. After various enquiries, in November 2009, two barristers (Anthony Temple QC and Peter Oliver, his junior) and a senior solicitor (Anthony Fincham), volunteered their help. They did this for the best reasons, wanting a fair hearing for a soldier who had died a difficult death in the course of duty, and I was very touched. They were to become a great support to me at a very difficult time.

Eventually, two half-day pre-inquest hearings were set up in Birmingham Coroner's Court in January and April 2010, nearly a year after Mark's death.

At these pre-hearings the MOD, David (acting for himself) and my lawyers made presentations to the Coroner about issues such as the breadth of the inquest, its length, whether a jury should be present: the Coroner would then decide. I realised then that because of its structure and process this inquiry was going to be adversarial, almost a fight, when I would have liked everyone to be working to the same end. I wondered if it should be such a battle when a soldier has died in the course of duty. Even Steve, my support officer, had a conflict of interest, representing the MOD whilst seeking to support me, and he was taken off the job just before the actual inquest hearing.

When we arrived at the first pre-hearing we were very surprised to be told that the Coroner had delegated it to a very competent deputy since he was unwell, that she would relay our submissions to him and he would then make the decisions; she could not decide. This bizarre process was completely irregular, but we felt we had no choice but to agree, or incur even more delay.

An important issue considered was whether the inquest should be an Article 2 inquest under the Human Rights Convention. At the time, this major legal matter was being debated by the House of Lords, the basic point being that the state has a duty, a responsibility, to look after its citizens wherever and under whatever circumstances they die, including war. Thus, in an Article 2 inquest the Coroner could be expected to consider not only how and when a person died, but also by what means and in what circumstances, and this would influence the witnesses called. My lawyers were keen that it was a broader Article 2 inquest; in contrast, the Army lawyers wanted as limited an inquiry as possible. Unfortunately, for some reason the Coroner chose not to clarify what type of inquest he was holding until during his summing up, which made the procedure more opaque.

The length of the inquest was also clearly important: it was a busy Coroner's court, soldiers and medical witnesses were to attend, and there might be a jury required. At the second pre-hearing, the Coroner initially suggested that the inquest might take well over a week, and twice as long if we had a jury. In the end, he decided that just four days without a jury in July 2010 should be booked in, and I wondered why it was to be less time than first discussed. Why no jury? He did not explain.

After these two pre-hearings, the Coroner asked the MOD lawyers to provide further specific information about the case, and so began several months of legal wrangling. The MOD initially agreed to send certain important documents but then reneged; some documents were never sent, but other documents the MOD said it could not find were subsequently found. Later, the disks said to contain documents arrived from Afghanistan but these disks were blank. Finally, a late document sent from Helmand turned out to be the order of the vigil memorial service held for Mark there, touching but irrelevant. The MOD did not make available the brigade-level watch keeper logs that were mentioned in the police report, logs of all activity from the brigade ops room. These logs were central to finding out how and when the helicopter had been requested and the reason for the delay. These 'chatroom' or 'J-chat' (so-called) documents undoubtedly did exist – parts of them were subsequently leaked to me independently – but the MOD could or would not find

them for the court. Despite all this, the Coroner felt able
to write a letter on 7 July 2010 to the parties concerned,
saying, 'In general, I have found the Ministry of Defence
disclose rather more than less than I would anticipate.'

The raw material for the inquest was to be the SIB
Military Police report, given to me in December 2009. It
was a substantial document, A4 size and about an inch
thick. Bizarrely, sensitive operational information had
been left in the report, to which we had to draw their
attention. It was initially so heavily redacted by the MOD
that it was almost impossible to understand and reading
it was extremely frustrating. Whole pages were missing,
names had been removed in an effort to anonymise the
document, but on the attached exhibits were the corre-
sponding initials, which painstakingly allowed the
witnesses' identification. We persuaded the MOD that
this document would not be a security threat if these details
were given. Over the next few weeks three differently
redacted versions were provided. These weighty documents had to be reread each time and then compared with
the original versions, a time-consuming, unnecessary and
inefficient process.

As well as the SIB report, the medical evidence was
extremely important. To understand the issues involved
one had to appreciate its complexity, which I am not sure
all involved did. Mark remained conscious in the patrol
base for about an hour after being shot and probably died
'medically' about twenty hours later in Bastion Hospital

when his pupils dilated, taken as a symptom of brain death. (A medical friend had read the medical notes for me as I felt unable to deal with these, with their graphic and impersonal descriptions: he had explained this to me.) We switched off his life support machines three days after his initial injury, the stopping of life being the legal date of death. Three reasons were given for Mark's death on the Coroner's interim death certificate of 21 May 2009: '… cause of death is 1(a) hypoxic brain injury 1(b) haemorrhage due to 1(c) gunshot wound to right shoulder (operated).'

Mark's '1(c) gunshot wound to the right shoulder' was serious, but innovative surgery meant that his body was in fact working when I first saw him, although he needed life support because the brain's means of messaging to the body had gone.

The '1(b) haemorrhage' was partly the result of the first surgery and also the gunshot wound. When he arrived at hospital there was no internal bleeding, but after the first operation he was returned to theatre for a second time to stop the internal bleeding caused by the first operation. Afterwards he had many hours of fluctuating blood pressure, needing more blood well into the night until finally the hospital blood supply was all used up. About this time his pupils dilated, the indicator that his brain was swelling. This in turn damaged the brain stem.

Thus the '1(a) hypoxic brain injury' or brain swelling

was caused by loss of blood, resulting in insufficient oxygen being delivered to the brain stem and brain and subsequent brain swelling. How long he had been bleeding and how much blood loss he had sustained before he received medical intervention at a hospital was clearly the main issue here.

Because the medical evidence was complex, my lawyers suggested that a trauma surgeon, Mr Matthews, be invited to advise us as an expert. Mr Matthews's report was based on the SIB report and the medical notes, and it was later used as evidence for the inquest. A letter written by Mark's Bastion Hospital surgeon, Lt Col Brooks, and dated 11 July 2010, was handed to the court and to us by the MOD lawyers just ten minutes before the start of proceedings. It was also used as evidence: we were given no time to consider it.

The head camera footage and other material supplied established the following important time frame:

8.42:   Injury.

8.46:   First nine-liner and request for help.

9.14:   Men arrive back at patrol base with Mark injured.

9.22:   Pedro (US helicopter) 35/36 were ready at BSN (Bastion).

9.25:   USA helicopter authorisation.

9.29:   Pedro/US Black Hawk helicopter takes off from Bastion.

9.32:   Mark can be heard saying, 'I am going down.' (In

the next few minutes Mark was moved to a side
room and needed CPR.)

9.47: Helicopter arrives; departs a minute later.

10.02 Mark arrives at Bastion Hospital for immediate
surgery.

As the time frame shows, Mark arrived back in the patrol
base at 9.14, conscious and speaking in sentences. He
was given a fluid injection by the team medic when the
latter got back, and he sat up and swore in reaction to
the pain. He was talking until he was put into a side room
at about 9.40, when he showed signs of deterioration and
was given CPR for breathing difficulties, talking little by
then. The helicopter finally arrived at 9.47. Thus he was
helicoptered out one hour after the initial nine-liner, just
beginning to show signs of coma.

Strangely this head camera footage was not shown in
open court. The Coroner only saw it privately one evening during the inquest, although the MOD had had it
for several months. The footage showed clearly the time
between the shout 'Man down' and Mark's last words,
and as such was important evidence when considering
questions about the timings and Mark's condition in the
patrol base as he lost consciousness. This footage was
not shown to the two medical experts whose evidence
was used.

So what happened at the inquest itself? It was held
in late July 2010, fifteen months after Mark's death, at

Sutton Coldfield Town Hall near Birmingham. It was an over-extended Victorian building with ochre walls and ornate features picked out in dark green, green-patterned carpets and cheap furnishings. Its crumbling damp walls and peeling wallpaper smelled of a lack of institutional care, and to me that was what the inquest came to be about.

In court the Coroner sat on a wooden throne in an alcove at the head of the large high-ceilinged room, surrounded by varnished woodwork announcing the Royal Town of Sutton Coldfield and listing all the mayors over many years.

At the beginning of proceedings and as a background, the entry dated 21 April in Mark's diary was read out, with his concern about the lack of radios, water, food and medical equipment, shortage of manpower and how safe they were.

The Welsh Guards Learning Account, written by Major Bettinson as a debriefing document for his superiors two days after the event and supplied to us beforehand by the MOD, explained what the unit was trying to do as it left on a routine patrol on 9 May: 'The tasks were to DOMINATE the surrounding terrain and DEMONSTRATE ISAF's [International Security Assistance Force] ability to provide security in the immediate AO [area of operation].'

The inquest then heard the written, or in some cases live, evidence of thirty-eight witnesses.

Some of the soldiers were present in the first two days of the inquest; the accounts of others were read from the SIB report. They brought home 'a harrowing tale of bravery and desperation', as Mr Matthews described it. Hearing the verbal accounts of the men was upsetting, for me and for them. They were stiff and uncomfortable in the court and afterwards told me that they could not bear it, the formal and impersonal account of that traumatic day, and they left as soon as they could. This bald inquisitorial legal process was trying to address a battle situation of great heroism, compassion and individual responsibility, and it felt very pale in comparison. The memories were ever-present for those soldiers, painful and demanding as they listened and spoke.

The soldiers were apparently briefed by Lt Col Kemp, responsible for co-ordinating all Army witnesses, a tough older soldier experienced with inquests. On the second day, some soldiers flew in from the Falklands and arrived late in the morning, without time to be briefed by him. I could see that their accounts were far more open and less inhibited (and in the end more useful for an understanding of the situation) than those who had been briefed by him the day before.

It was an old court, and the witnesses stood on a small dais between the Coroner and the rows of seats in the public area of the court. Directly in front of them were Lt Col Kemp and then the MOD legal representatives. On the second day, Mark's father David angrily pointed out to the Coroner that soldiers on the witness stand could clearly be seen frequently glancing at Lt Col Kemp, as if checking that their answers were acceptable. This apparent influencing of witnesses was obvious to David, an artist inexperienced in legal matters, and it was quite clear to many present. David formally questioned Lt Col Kemp about this, and he denied it by explaining the importance of the control of security issues. The Coroner chose not to deal with the matter further, justifying the situation to David, who found this very hard to accept.

Dr Nicholas Hunt, the highly respected Home Office consultant pathologist who had carried out the autopsy, gave evidence in the course of the first day. The only part of his evidence that really upset me was hearing him emphasise in this public place that Mark had 'bled to death'. That statement by a medical person brought home to me the reality of what Mark had suffered, its actuality rather than my imagination. He slowly bled, conscious most of the time, whilst he waited for a helicopter to take him to hospital. One could hardly imagine the trauma and pain of this.

Newspapers that first evening wrote of the inadequate medical kit available at the time of injury, and that the soldiers had yet to be issued HEMCON bandages. Implicit in these articles was the cause of a great deal of upset for the men as they tried to 'make do'. (The Coroner later agreed with the medical experts that that this made little difference, Mark needed operative care.)

On the third day more witness accounts were read, and Major Henry Bettinson gave oral evidence as the senior officer representing the Army. (Captain Chris Lambe told me later that he attended the inquest for a day and offered to speak as a witness, since he had been Mark's HQ radio contact during the incident. But this important offer was not taken up by the MOD lawyers and strikingly was not communicated to mine. Had we been told of his involvement at the time we would have pressed for him to be called.)

On the fourth day, the Coroner summed up and gave his verdict. (See Appendix II for a complete transcript.)

Over the previous months the senior lawyer acting for me had mastered the complexity of the case, whereas the Coroner, who was legally but not medically trained, sometimes appeared challenged by it. The fact of the different levels of preparation was evident through the hearing.

The evidence over the three days was called by the Coroner under two main headings: 'Bowman Radio' and 'Medical Evidence and Helicopter Delay' (covering similar issues, helicopter delay and its impact on Mark's survival).

When discussing the Bowman radio and communications problems, Major Bettinson said, almost as a self-evident truth, that in the situation in which they were, radios were more powerful and important than guns. Mark had been shot in the back moving from a doorway in which he had been trying to get a proper signal and see what was happening 'eyes on'. He needed communication with the rest of the platoon and HQ during an ambush so dangerous that he must have thought that all his soldiers could die in that hot, barren, strange place.

The soldiers described in their evidence how 'comms' or radio contact was a 'constant drama'. Some soldiers spoke about the dampening effect of their ECM radios, designed to confuse the enemy signal but dangerously interfering with their own Bowman radio signals, evidence which made Lt Col Kemp agitated. The MOD press officer later actively discouraged the press from reporting the possible effect of these radios on Mark's radio signal.

As they realised the extent of the ambush, neither Mark nor the Fire Support Team (100 m away) could call down air support that would have normally frightened the Taleban away. LBdr Spooner's Bowman radio was unable to communicate directly with the fire support helicopter, his satellite radio had been disabled, and the radio 'relay' for fire support through Silab was just too slow and difficult in the heat of battle.

Thus, at this time the senior members of the patrol had variable reception with HQ for their VHR Bowman radios, some signals were perhaps being affected by the ECM devices carried by some soldiers, the patrol had no useful contact with the fire support helicopter, and their interpersonal PRR radios had not been given to all soldiers on patrol.

Major Bettinson's Learning Account, dated 9 May 2009, explained:

Communications between the ground c/s and PB SLB [Patrol Base Silab] were difficult throughout the TIC [troops in combat] … These must be more robust now. They are unsustainable, hinder the ability to pass information upwards and HAJper [sic. hamper?] the ability to allocate additional resources to the TIC. This continues to be my greatest concern. [He went on to identify problems with charging batteries in that patrol base.]

FST [Fire Support Team] A patrol should not deploy on the ground without satisfactory communications on the TFH [Task Force Helmand] STRIKE Net. This is a GO/NO GO criterion … No patrol will deploy on the ground without a FST component that has good communications on the TFH STRIKE net.

The risk versus reward of deploying 300 m beyond CP HAJ [PB Haji-Alem] has been reconsidered in the light of this incident. This issue will be discussed with Comd Offr BG [Commanding Officer Battlegroup] (CS) this week.

While the commander will continue to try to out think the INS [insurgents] in this area, it will remain challenging to avoid pattern setting due to the large fields of view, the obstacles immediately outside the CP and its exposed position. The location would benefit from an increase in combat power and improved communications.

Thus he was acknowledging the importance of these communications problems and also of not going on patrol in the future without easy access to the fire support helicopters.

Astonishingly, despite what the men said there under oath, despite what he had written in the Learning Account shortly after the events, and notwithstanding a letter from the Company Adjutant describing the communications problems at the time, when he was there in court giving evidence Major Bettinson dismissed the significance of the radio communications problems. To our surprise, he sought to explain the inconsistency between his statement in court and his own Learning Account by saying that he had written the latter incorrectly in a state of emotional distress following the death of a close colleague. For me, it was a revelatory moment: was he just speaking for the MOD or was he a witness for the situation at the time? The conflict was there for all to see.

The Coroner had this to say about communications in his summing up:

This is a particularly significant area as it is partly the reason why Mark was in the position he was when he was shot. It is clear from the evidence that he was in that position partly because he wanted to get 'eyes on' and partly because he was trying to get signals on his radio. It was for these reasons that he went to the entrance knowing he was exposed and taking a risk. He needed to talk to Lance Sergeant Peek and Company Command. This was an extremely brave thing to do. He was under constant fire. Mark must have known the risks he faced. We do not know if he was not receiving any signal on his radio or just that the reception was poor. I remind you that it is not the purpose of the inquest to enquire into whether Bowman is the appropriate radio for the British Army, nor to find out if the British Army have enough of these radios or if the Electronic Counter Measures interfere with the Bowman radios. That is a political matter to be debated by Parliament. My concern is how or whether it impacted on Mark's death.

If Mark had been sent out on patrol without a radio or with a broken radio, that would be a matter of great concern. We heard yesterday that one soldier said that ECM blocked the Bowman radio whilst other soldiers said that it did not. The others said that other things affected the Bowman, examples being the terrain or the weather. We know as a fact that the platoon was having trouble with the radios on the patrol. What we need to know is if Mark had a dud radio or whether he was just suffering temporary problems. I think it is safe to assume that Lt Evison would have checked his radio before going out on patrol. From what I have heard of him, I can't imagine he would have gone out without doing so. I am also sure that if he was taking a patrol out and whilst he was out he had significant radio problems, he would have not continued with the patrol. We have heard that he was using his radio during the thirty minutes before he was wounded. This came out of the evidence of the soldiers, the log book records and from Major Bettinson, who says he received communications from Lt Evison at 8.28, 8.32, 8.35 and 8.38.

It is likely that Mark was shot at 8.42 or around that time. Guardsman Tucker then used his radio successfully a few minutes after he fell. Tucker spoke to Company Command without difficulty. Tucker said in his statement that he saw Guardsman James treating Lt Evison and that he picked up Lt Evison's radio and informed Company Command of the casualty. He said he also heard Lance Sergeant Peek requesting help over the radio to get the platoon out of the compounds. I therefore conclude from the evidence that it is more likely than not that Mark Evison's Bowman radio was working but had temporary problems with the signal and that was one of the reasons why Mark moved into the doorway of the compound.

We have heard that there were difficulties with Personal Role Radios. However, in the evidence that we have heard, there have been frequent references to speaking on the Personal Role Radios. I am not saying that they did not have problems from time to time, however, it would be wrong to say they had no communications, just that they were sometimes ineffective.

It is clear that the Coroner was not prepared to look at the broader question of whether inadequate communications had contributed to Mark's death. But this is precisely what an Article 2 inquest should address, as other Coroners have in other inquests. Was it good enough that the radios which were sometimes ineffective were used? Should they not have been supplied with radios which worked, enough interpersonal radios and spares for broken radios?

Turning to his summary of medical treatment, the Coroner stated (italics are as given in his written verdict, I have highlighted some in bold for emphasis):

Neglect in a Coroner's court constitutes gross failure to provide medical attention to a dependent person and there **must be a causative link to the person's death**. It doesn't need to be the main or only cause, it **just has to be a contributing cause.**

I have had to consider the involvement of Guardsman James, Corporal Lacy, Guardsman Korosaya, Gunner Gadsby, Guardsman Richards, Guardsman Hobbs and the Afghan National Army Soldier who carried Mark's stretcher. I have also had to consider the people who administered treatment at the patrol base, in the helicopter, at Camp Bastion, and during the flight back to the UK and Selly Oak Hospital.

Coroners work on the basis of a balance of probabilities. **It is clear that Mark received a very serious wound, which in the circumstances in which it was sustained was more likely than not to result in his death despite all the heroic efforts of his men and of the surgeons at Camp Bastion** … I do not find neglect in any medical attention. No one ever suggested that I should record such a finding. No one has expressed concern about the treatment that Mark received at Camp Bastion or at Selly Oak Hospital. Mr Matthews said that the treatment received at Camp Bastion was indeed remarkable and it was a testament to the treatment received that he had survived so long. He described their efforts at Camp Bastion as nothing short of heroic. I believe that this comment is justified.

The Coroner did not mention that Mark had been doing quite well for almost an hour and that had the helicopter not been delayed, he could have been in hospital whilst still conscious and breathing. He drew his conclusion from two medical experts, neither of whom was aware of the timings or of Mark's condition at 9.15.

The Coroner went on to say:

We know that Mark's injury was originally assessed by the soldiers as a Category C injury when it should have been a Category B injury. **I am entirely satisfied that this wrong categorisation did not contribute to Mark's death.** Colonel Kemp, I would like you to make it clear to the relevant soldiers that this did not contribute to Mark's death.

The Coroner's assessment concluded:

Colonel Kemp, please can you speak to Guardsman James and Corporal Lacy and ensure that they understand that there is nothing they could have done to save Mark's life. I am not satisfied that they appreciate that.

There was no further discussion of this: witnesses who could speak for the effect of a change in categorisation of the injury on the helicopter delay were not called. The Coroner here refers only to the shoulder injury, apparently ignoring Mark's brain injury.

We knew that Mr Matthews did not hear the soldiers give evidence at the inquest as he only attended court for a short period on the second day for questioning. The surgeon Lt Col Brooks knew little of Mark's medical condition before arriving at Bastion Hospital, at what point Mark had needed CPR and how long the process of his being recovered in the field had taken. Thus neither had seen or heard evidence of before and when Mark finally lost consciousness, including the video footage. Yet the Coroner summed up the issues around the helicopter delay as follows. (Again, I have highlighted some in bold):

Lieutenant Colonel Brooks agrees that nothing could have been done to stop the bleeding other than by way of surgical intervention but he disagrees that at the time that CPR was administered, Mark's life could not have been saved. Lieutenant Colonel Brooks goes on to say that there is a mortality rate of 50 per cent with those presenting with relatively stable vital signs with this injury at a Unit 1 Trauma Unit. In the circumstances in which Mark sustained his wounds, the mortality rate approaches 100 per cent. Where there is difficulty in extracting the casualty and there is a history of the need for cardiopulmonary resuscitation, the chances of surviving even if the injury was to happen on a doorstep of a hospital in the UK are negligible. Should injury occur on the doorstop of a Level 1 Trauma Unit, there would be a small chance of survival.

The delay to the authorisation of the helicopter has variously been referred to as thirty-two minutes, thirty-seven minutes and thirty-nine minutes. I will refer to it as thirty-nine minutes as this appears to be the time from the nine-liner to the time when the authorisation was given, the time of the nine-liner being 8.46 and the time of the authorisation for the helicopter being 9.25. Mrs Evison is understandably concerned about this delay and **neither the Army nor the inquest has been able to explain it.**

My concern for this inquest is **whether it is more likely**

than not that this contributed to his death. I do not believe so. I rely on paragraph 54 of Mr Matthews's report:

'From the witness statements it is not clear to me exactly the state of Lieutenant Evison at quarter past nine. This I believe is a matter for the inquest to determine but if his pulse was becoming un-recordable and required ventilator support by bagging or by cardiopulmonary resuscitation at that time, whilst intravenous resuscitation may have been administered in the helicopter, it would have not been possible to stop the bleeding during the helicopter journey and indeed, as it happened he went into full cardio-pulmonary arrest during the helicopter flight and I am of the opinion that at the stage he was requiring cardiopulmonary resuscitation, as a consequence to blood loss, that Lieutenant Evison's life could not effectively be saved, despite the tempo-rary success of heroic attempts to do so.'

Mr Matthews also said in paragraph 57 of his report:

*'The guidance I can give the inquest is that I am of the opinion that by the time Lieutenant Mark Evison was beginning to drift in and out of consciousness, he was unsal-vageable without advanced resuscitative techniques. **By the time he required cardiopulmonary support, on the balance of probabilities, long-term survival was not a realistic expectation and even if that were not so, the hypoxic brain injury in association with this state of affairs, would have rendered him requiring care and support for the rest of his life, possibly in a persistent vegetative state.'***

Lieutenant Colonel Brooks comments on the delay to the helicopter of thirty-two or thirty-seven minutes, as variously recorded:

'It is unproven and conjecture that if Lieutenant Evison had received surgical intervention thirty-two minutes earlier that it would have altered the outcome. In my opinion the suggested "32-minute delay" had minimal impact on the chance of survival ... The injury occurred in a military contact in Afghanistan, within this context the chance of survival of this injury are minimal. However, I believe that it was correct to make all efforts possible as done.'

Lt Col Brooks was entitled to his opinion, but it must be the case that the longer the period before the bleeding is controlled the higher the possibility of mortality. It was common sense – the longer the delay the worse the outcome.

As the Coroner presented it, Lt Col Brooks seemed confused about the possibility of survival, mentioning a mortality rate of 50 per cent and then a sentence later, approaching 100 per cent. The Coroner did not indicate specifically the reasons for this variation.

Lt Col Brooks disagreed with aspects of Mr Matthews's initial report, mostly over the issue of local trauma experience and results at Bastion Hospital. His caution was mirrored by Dr Nicholas Hunt, who in the SIB report was careful to state:

The survivability of the initial vascular injuries must be viewed in the context in which the injuries occurred rather than making inappropriate comparisons with expectations for survival in a civilian setting at a top flight trauma facility. Indeed from a pathological perspective the fact that he survived so long bears a testament to the quality of the immediate care he received in the field.

He clearly knew of the innovative, ground-breaking work that would be done in such a field hospital on young men at the peak of their strength and fitness. Yet at the inquest some conclusions were fundamentally based on precisely such comparisons with other services and other age groups, with little reference to the quality of the care in the field.

I knew that the Americans did not classify Mark's particular type of shoulder injury in the field as fatal but as potentially survivable, and that another lieutenant, Tom Spencer Smith, had sustained a similar shoulder injury slightly later in the campaign and had survived to return to duties. He had been helicoptered out forty minutes after being shot and had not developed the same hypoxic brain swelling.

Mr Matthews had invited the court to differentiate Mark's condition at 9.15, when he had recently arrived at the patrol base, from his condition when he left half an hour later, helicoptered out. He also said (paragraph 48 of his report): 'Had Lt Evison arrived at the shock room of a level one trauma unit at the point where his pulse was quite slow and drifting in and out of consciousness, **he may perhaps have been salvageable**.' He clearly did not think the SIB report was clear enough about the medical state Mark was in both at 9.15 and half an hour later, and specifically asked the inquest to look at Mark's condition at these times. He put the onus on the Coroner to sort this out. If the Coroner had seen the head camera footage by this time he should have understood this and followed it up. The evidence from the head camera and the soldiers suggested that Mark had begun to lose consciousness around 9.40 – that was when he began drifting in and out of consciousness and needed CPR. Before that he was talking clearly to the men, albeit somewhat drowsy on some morphine. Yet this request of Mr Matthews to look at Mark's condition at 9.15 was ignored, and the Coroner did not ask the soldiers these questions.

Whilst the Coroner was not prepared to look at reasons for the helicopter delay, despite its being an Article 2 inquest, I was aware that the SIB report suggested three different possible reasons for it. The Coroner said specifically that the confusion around the upgrading of his injury from Category C to Category B, with the subsequent conflicting radio messages, did not contribute to the delay, although the report gave this as a possible reason. An explanation given to the men, also stated in the police report, was that a British Chinook helicopter had initially been sent incorrectly or sent to another base to pick up an injured civilian before Mark. This seems unlikely, since a Chinook was known to JHC to be too large to land at Mark's patrol base, but this possibility was not discussed in court. The third reason given to the men at the time, that there were no medical helicopters available, was not discussed.

The Learning Account makes no mention of other helicopter demand and activity but registers an 8.46 nine-liner and the Pedro (American Black Hawk medical helicopter) being available at 9.22. It seemed to me that with anguished requests coming from the men from around 9 a.m., a request for an American helicopter would have been made earlier if it was clear that the Chinook had gone elsewhere, was too big to land in the patrol base and could not land in a battle. If helicopter command made that request, what happened to it? Why was a representative of helicopter command not invited to the inquest to explain, to give evidence? Why did the MOD not retrieve the relevant logs? What happened to those requests? These questions were not addressed.

Thus the inquest made no attempt to relate Mark's condition to the helicopter delay. Mr Matthews's recommendations to the court that this needed to be done should have been followed through. The Coroner's conclusions again were drawn without the appropriate evidence being considered. And although the Coroner said that members of his profession worked on the basis of probabilities, nevertheless the doctors explained that the medical world is one of opinion, and the possibility of working with low odds is acceptable.

Mark did survive his shoulder injury, although one can never know if he would have survived the internal haemorrhaging and damage to his internal organs as a result of the radical surgery. It seems that there would have been time for him to arrive conscious at Bastion Hospital before 9.40 if the helicopter had been there as requested, notwithstanding a fourteen-minute helicopter trip. If he had arrived at Bastion Hospital still conscious and before he needed radical surgery, before his heart was 'dry' (i.e. unable to sustain adequate cerebral perfusion), if his shoulder wound had been clamped and fluids given immediately, surely his brain swelling may have been less of a risk, not happening as it did until about twenty hours later? If he had arrived then, such serious surgery might not have been required and its consequent internal haemorrhaging could have been avoided.

Despite all this, Mark gave up his life very unwillingly, he was a fit young man in the prime of his life – one of the fittest in the Army – and he was used to trying. He was perhaps more likely to survive than most. This needed to be factored in and was not – and that he tried so hard to remain conscious until the end.

The Coroner continued:

I take the point of Mr Temple QC that there is always a chance of survival and that any delay must diminish the chances of survival however minimal. I do not think it's right to move from that position to say that the delay caused his death.

My lawyers were never arguing that the delay *caused* Mark's death, as the Coroner's observation implied. Owing to the curious rules governing inquests a party to the inquest may ask questions but not make a speech. Our position in the pre-hearings before the inquest had been that its contribution needed investigation and evaluation.

In his summing up, the Coroner thoughtfully said that if after the inquest the MOD found material explaining the reason for the delay, it should be sent on to the family:

Mrs Evison is understandably concerned about this delay and neither the Army nor the inquest has been able to explain it. I am satisfied that the Army did try to help and that if the documents become available, they will tell the parents and the court.

The Coroner's lack of understanding of the MOD lawyers was now plain for us to see. Sadly, the somewhat brutal response to my lawyers' request for this material after the inquest was:

As the inquest is now concluded the MOD does not propose to engage in a further specific search for documents which may or may not exist, as it does not consider that it has an obligation to do so.

A secondary issue that came up during the proceedings was that of the 'golden hour', long used in previous wars as a rule of thumb to aim for when saving soldiers' lives in battle. Mr Matthews observed, as a trauma surgeon, that the minimum two-hour time frame from injury to urgent treatment was inadequate to save men's lives: he said that the 'golden hour' should be aimed for, and preferably recovery of the injured should be quicker, as soon as possible. This 'golden hour' is not now NATO policy, and Major Bettinson in his Learning Account expressed himself as satisfied that 'in this case the casualty reached surgical intervention within one hour and twenty minutes – well within the timeline for Cat B'. Such complacency is unacceptable if the objective is to save lives. If Mark had been retrieved within the 'golden hour' it is just possible that he would be here today.

As to the important question of the breadth and parameters of the inquest, the Coroner said: 'I hope you will give me credit that I have carried out a full investigation into the identity of the deceased, how and by what means he came by his death.' He did not mention looking into 'in what circumstances', thus implying it was not an Article 2 inquest. But in his summing up at the end of the inquest he concluded:

I have told you that I have carried out an Article 2 investigation. The focus must be and has been on Mark. My concern as Coroner is not what medical supplies troops should carry or if they had whether it would have saved his life. It is not that the British Army should pledge to extract men who have been injured within what has been described as the 'golden hour'. My concern is should Mark have got to an operating theatre quickly, would it have saved his life? My concern is not with Bowman radios' compatibility with ECM. It is whether Mark had a Bowman radio and whether it was working as well as can be expected. The other things are political decisions to be decided by Parliament. I am quite sure if the government set up a public inquiry, I would be very surprised if they turned to me to comment on those issues.

This was a rather confused summary. In it he clearly made assumptions about 'what could be expected' with regard to radios. But the Coroner also said that he had carried out an Article 2 inquest. If this was the case, it was very surprising that he did not ask beforehand for the appropriate witnesses to attend who could have addressed some of the major wider issues. The fact that he did not invite them implied that he was not planning for a comparatively wide-ranging inquiry. Had he or had he not conducted a wider inquest? It may be that the Coroner's lack of understanding of the subtleties of the arguments put to him (and indirectly through his deputy) in the pre-hearings led to his failure to call the appropriate evidence for the case, or there may have been other pressures.

I am aware that as the mother of a dead soldier, I could stand accused of being embittered, and wanting a rerun or reconsideration of the proceedings because of my unhappiness with them, when this unhappiness may stem largely from grief or be distorted by it. But the facts were there. Why did the Coroner fail to ensure there was proper disclosure of documents? How could he investigate the reasons for Mark's death without calling the relevant witnesses? Why did he not invite further medical experts to comment on Mark's neurological condition, or even really acknowledge it in court as a cause of death? Why were experts and witnesses not shown the head camera footage with its clear time frame for Mark's physical deterioration? Why were the soldiers not asked to describe Mark's condition at 9.15, and again at 9.45? Why was the Coroner so keen to arrange for a much shorter inquest without a jury? Finally, how could the Coroner claim to have conducted a wider Article 2 inquest and at the same time fail to call evidence, effectively limiting the extent of the evidence on the basis that 'Mark would have died anyway'? The two concepts are incompatible.

There seemed to me a fundamental illogicality in the argument that Mark would have died anyway. At the time Mark was being treated, the medical team did not know that his death would eventually take place; otherwise they might not have tried so hard. I understood the principle of triage used in hospitals, by which only salvageable serious cases are operated on in order to protect resources. Clearly they used a considerable amount of resources for Mark: they were prepared to use all the blood supplies available trying to save him, to try six hours of innovative and complex surgery, and the doctor spent all night at his bedside. On that Saturday the clinical team must have believed he could survive or they would not have continued. All those there believed it was possible: the padre had told me so. When I was told the category of Mark's injury on 9 May it was not suggested to me that he would be unlikely to survive (that category would have been VVSI or fatal wound, whereas Mark's wound was called VSI or very serious injury). Hindsight is not appropriate in this case. The circumstances of Mark's death at the time should have been under investigation at the inquest, the time when they assumed he may survive. Even if there was a low probability of survival at the moment of injury these issues needed investigation and explanation. He was not dead yet.

Ultimately, what does one make of the apparently empty process of the inquest? This death was perhaps preventable, and in the end Mark bled until his heart was 'dry' only 20–30 km from a sophisticated hospital base. That was a travesty of the Military Covenant, and no explanation was forthcoming. Was this good enough for other serving soldiers?

At a personal level, the process seemed to trivialise Mark's death, rubberstamping it, the 'final sacrifice' somehow cheapened. It tainted how I felt about the Army, my loss and Mark's legacy; it set me back in how I recovered from his death. I was left with the disappearance (as I saw it then) of this very loved person with only partial explanation or answers. This was a far cry from the 'closure' that my support officer Steve had told me that the inquest should bring.

It seemed wrong to me that this inquest, an 'inquiry', this process of justice in a court with opposing barristers and all its trappings, the summing up and the verdict, was in the hands of one man. The Coroner was not a judge, although he was performing a quasi-judicial function. He announced his exhaustion during the inquest, and he was absent for the first pre-hearing and clearly unwell at the second pre-hearing, with coughing fits which halted proceedings. With one person in charge, listening and deciding, his expertise and state of mind were clearly important. He discouraged the appointment of a jury, which in retrospect could have resulted in a better standard of inquiry. He made it clear that he believed it would be better if he controlled the process – perhaps it was routine for him, he was doing his job as he knew how. He said that with a jury it would take twice as long, and there was evidently little court time available.

The Coroner was clearly sympathetic to the rigours of war, keen that the soldiers were reassured that they had done everything right. In contrast, when my ex-husband complained about the proximity of the witness being examined to a senior officer, the Coroner seemed remarkably unresponsive, refusing to see it as an issue. Throughout the proceedings I was also surprised by the attitude of MOD officials to me as a parent. It was a terrible moment when the MOD barrister suggested to me that the doctors had expressed a little hope in those anguished four days just because they were 'trying to be nice to me', implying that they knew otherwise whilst they tried to save Mark's life.

As events had unfolded at the inquest, there developed a sense of 'whitewash', initially with the process of obtaining information and then with the Coroner's summing up and verdict. Then afterwards I felt angry, the anger of frustration at injustice, at hidden powers seeming to control and dictate. This was the first time I had felt anger about Mark's death.

After the inquest was over, I understood the anger of other families. I sympathised with and supported the recent British Legion's campaign on behalf of bereaved families to appoint a Chief Coroner. It was latterly successful, and Mr Kenneth Clarke, the Justice Secretary, announced in 2011 that under the new plan a Chief Coroner will now be 'focusing on working to deliver the reform to the Coroners' service that we want to see', with 'the full range of powers to drive up standards, including Coroner training, as well as setting minimum standards of service', and 'better treatment for bereaved families'.

But however trained and empowered the Coroner will be, with the present structure of military inquests still in place the MOD lawyers will continue to be there. The MOD approach to this process will be paramount, an approach which in my view needs a thorough review.

Later, I reflected on the broader picture, why the MOD behaved as it did. It is known to be a secretive controlling institution, resistant to change and fearful of being sued, perhaps because in its case admitting fault can have major financial implications across the whole Armed Forces. For example, a return to the 'golden hour' rule for getting the injured to hospital has recently been reintroduced by the Americans with significant savings in life but at considerable cost. Sadly there were perhaps limits to the MOD's care for its troops, and Mark's lingering death may well have been a consequence of this and thus an embarrassment to the organisation.

What other explanations could there be for the MOD's obfuscations when asked to provide information, nearly a year after Mark's death? Was the MOD being inefficient or secretive, or was there a darker explanation? Was it possible that the MOD had attempted to achieve a verdict that ensured its own culpability in the widest sense for unnecessary deaths was not examined? It appeared that it had acted to avoid a detailed inquiry into its own systemic failings, to me representing a major moral, political and legal question.

In September 2010, just before the long-awaited Defence Spending Review, I had watched with horror a Channel 4 *Dispatches* programme on equipment and financial waste in the Armed Forces and MOD, waste which had the effect of limiting the funds available to soldiers in the field. A journalist rang who had been long aware of the head camera footage that I had been given, and who knew that I had been previously unwilling to release it; but this time I said yes, I would release it. The MOD tried to stop me, threatening me with an injunction. I heard no more about this as soon as my lawyers pointed out that this material had been publicly available and considered at the inquest.

On 5 October 2010 Channel 4 used this footage for its main news item of the day. (Subsequently, the journalist concerned, Kris Jepson, was nominated for the Young Journalist of the Year Award.) It gave a detailed account of what had happened. For the first time people could see and understand how it had felt for the men with their beloved commanding officer and friend in their arms as they waited for a helicopter. Jepson pointed out that the questions surrounding the helicopter delay and aspects of Mark's death had still not been answered by the MOD. The current Conservative Prime Minister, David Cameron, was interviewed immediately afterwards, and was shown saying, 'For too long we did not have enough helicopters in Afghanistan.' Was he implicitly acknowledging that the problem that day was a shortage of helicopters?

The MOD issued a press statement in response to this programme, saying:

> Our sympathies remain with Mrs Evison following the death of her son Lt Mark Evison. The independent Coroner concluded that the time taken for the medical helicopter to arrive did not contribute to Lt Evison's death as his injuries were, sadly, unsurvivable. The inquest also heard that the radios were working and an extensive log of the patrol communications were shared with the Coroner.

There could not have been one person who heard the evidence at the inquest, or one soldier who was there with Mark at the time, who could honestly say that the radios were 'working' in any real sense. The evidence was that communications were sporadic at best, and that communications problems were a major issue that day and for a large part of the tour, and significantly influenced the calling down of air support which could have saved the situation. The MOD's response was stereotypical, frightening in its lack of moral integrity, that most important and central Army value. That response in itself emphasised the huge gulf between this fighting Army and its master. It allowed no consideration and institutional change, and in that sense Mark's seemed a wasted death, just another statistic.

CHAPTER 9

IMPRESSIONS OF AFGHANISTAN AND THE WAR

I seem to be the only one here who believes that war might not be the answer to this particular problem. We must work on relationships with the Afghanis if we are to build a future for them. Maybe my perspective will change in the next few days and weeks.

Extract from Mark's diary, 28 April 2009

Only a week after the Coroner's inquest I found myself, by a strange twist of fate, in a local Afghan aeroplane looking down on the lumpy brown eiderdown of mountains outside Kabul, stretching on and on into a distance far away. The plane hugged those peaks, almost too closely. My companion told me cheerfully that planes occasionally fly into them, the wreckage and bodies hard to retrieve because of the mines peppered through the steep slopes. We flew over valleys and could see the little high-walled family compounds and the patchwork of irrigation ditches bordering brown fields, now familiar from the video footage I had seen. It looked a harsh and alien environment, a long way from the ordered gentle green of Mark's childhood. I was overcome by deep sadness, a melancholy hard to shake off: here he had died in this strange place too far from home.

So why was I here? Mark's death may have shocked the Army and given it pause for thought. It was one of many that were slowly making the British public question what our boys were doing there, as I had done throughout this time. But just sixteen months after his death I still wanted to find Mark, to be closer to where he had died, to know what he had seen, almost to be with him. I wanted to see what he had died for, to comfort myself that his death had a worth or a meaning in some way – that perhaps a country or people had benefited. I thought that going to Afghanistan might help me make sense of the sacrifice of these young British lads.

The trip had been offered as an auction prize at an Army ball several months before. The moment I heard of it I knew that I wanted to go. I was aware that the trip might be dangerous, that Elizabeth had just lost her brother and was vulnerable to any further tragedy, but she said she understood why I should go and even encouraged me.

My journey's beginnings were not auspicious. I lost my passport before travelling and decided to go to the airport without it. I was turned away, I had to find it; that took several hours. It had been kicked under a bed, and was finally retrieved by Elizabeth after the flight had left without me. We managed to find another flight, but were then directed to the wrong airport. So we turned back, the taxi racing across south London to catch the flight. After many hours of high drama and racking tension I was there. But my luggage was lost en route, not to reappear until it was time to come home.

We were to travel to Kabul, the capital far in the east, and then to Bamiyan and the Panshir valley, all peaceful areas now free from the Taleban. Sadly the south, including Helmand where had Mark died, is too dangerous for tourists. Sandy Gall led the trip, an 84-year-old journalist who knew the country well and who had been an important political commentator at the time of the Mujahedeen; he had even set up a charity there, making prostheses for locals injured as a result of war. Major General Peter Gilchrist, now retired, told me he had worked there in Kabul in 2006 under the Americans and subsequently in Washington. He was fascinated by the country and wanted to show it to his wife. Charles Moore, a respected senior journalist, and his wife were curious to find out more about the country. Kate was an intrepid young artist. Over the days their personalities and experience played out with the tensions as we had to deal with floods, cancelled planes, taxis that strangely did not take us the way we expected to go. All of us were carrying a fear of the potential risks, of kidnap and even murder. We shared clothes, food, toothpaste, cameras, scarves and danger; some gin carried in Sandy's suitcases helped, offering a calm end to each day.

We drove in from Kabul airport along wide potholed streets, heaving with 4x4s, trucks and old cars. It was chaotic – there were few traffic lights and only occasional police in the centre of busy intersections trying to control the traffic, which was dominated by frustrated hooting and pushing. Some bicycle riders dared venture into the fray, lithe young men or turbaned older Afghans in flowing robes on rickety steeds. There were only a few motorbikes, which were the precious property of the more moneyed young men. I was told that there were no traffic offences here because there was no justice system to enforce them. Courts had the capacity to deal only with serious crime: drug smuggling, terrorism, murder. I knew that security was often quoted as the reason for the British Army being there, and here one could see a hint of the magnitude of the problem.

The streets were lined with ramshackle stalls selling melons and lush produce from the irrigated valleys. There were only a few small trees, perhaps too young to cut down for all-important firewood or only recently planted. Footpaths were busy but there were only very few women, faceless in their blue billowing silk burkas. Men in the streets looked handsome with their stern unsmiling gazes. To smile was considered sexually provocative: it implied a familiarity unachieved as yet, a strictly Western custom. Yet the men were often demonstrably affectionate with each other and stood in groups talking.

The city felt derelict in many ways. Buildings with harsh and bare-faced concrete walls were usually guarded by Afghan police with large guns. Often I saw the remaining walls of rubble buildings peppered with bullet marks and then, just occasionally, relics of an elegant and cultured past. Our hotel, Gandamack Lodge, was unannounced on the street and set back behind two pairs of armed guards and heavy metal doors: one entered after eye slots were opened and cars had been checked for possible explosives. Inside it was a green oasis with a garden of grass, vines and fruit trees.

It rained for the first two days in Kabul, making the smaller streets almost impassable with mud. As I was without my baggage, I went to the local bazaar with a guide to buy some new clothes, pretty cheap cotton things with long sleeves and long skirts. I was warned to walk the streets very cautiously, and I was shocked by the constant sense of danger. Security was a fairly new anxiety. One could feel and see the effects of thirty years of war, with the Russians, the Mujahedeen, the Taleban and now the Western forces. I was told it had been a sophisticated city in the 1970s, a city where Afghanistan had met the West, but now it seemed stripped of culture and history. It felt an unhappy city to me: if there was contentedness and liveliness it happened behind closed or locked doors. Perhaps the city was still recovering after being taken from the Taleban in 2001, going forward rather than going back, but I could not tell.

Later we drove through areas of shanty town away from the centre. Rising up in the pale brown hills behind were layers of mud-brick homes, unpainted, and some wide treeless stony areas with large dogs running wild. Large billboards spoke for Western communication systems, road rules, chicken stock cubes and political candidates for the coming election. We passed the huge and ornate Dunya Wedding Hall, only surpassed in splendour by the mosques. The snow-fed Kabul River was littered and almost dry in August, although usually occasional irrigation systems allowed some cultivation of nearby fields. Just once we saw boys playing football and cricket in a sports ground, a reminder of a young wish to play, but I saw little of that.

We visited Kabul museum, and outside a boy of about nine came up, cheeky, taunting us for 'just looking', and said we would be better off spending our time praying. What he saw were tourists wasting their time, and I could sense his palpable dislike of us: this was his country, we were strangers and tourism was a threat. Sadly, inside the museum there was very little, it had been looted and stripped of nearly all its pieces when the Taleban held Kabul. Amongst the remaining works were some beautiful Buddhist pieces from the third and fourth centuries, and a collection of animistic and polytheistic works from Nuristan, north-east Afghanistan, made by Kafirs or non-believers, relics of an Indo-Iranian past. I was surprised that these were dated towards the end of the eighteenth century, and that such simple figures should be the art of such recent times, they seemed unsophisticated pieces.

This was Kabul, the capital, stripped and tense, and I looked forward to visiting a country region closer to the life Mark might have seen. The country is divided at many levels, into provinces and also by tribal intolerance and hatred, and as well by the religious differences between Sunni and Shia Muslims. The southern Pashtun sprawl out over the border of Pakistan, whilst the Northern Alliance encompasses a group of northern tribes. The Taleban and President Karzai are Pashtun, a deeply conservative tribe. These tribal and religious tensions were palpable, part of life here.

By chance at breakfast I met Norine, a woman living in the hotel but with a house in Lashkar Gah also. She was interviewing locals to produce ground-level research for ICOS, a small policy think tank. She explained to me why the situation was difficult and the war slow to be effective in that deeply conservative southern region. The country had so little at a national level: education only locally (only 20 per cent reading and writing nationally and less in the south), no medicine, no voting system, and only a skeletal judicial system and army. The south was the most war-torn and dangerous, but the locals knew that the Western forces would soon leave and so their own ultimate survival was their main preoccupation. Schools built by the Armed Forces in Helmand were then deserted or destroyed, no teachers or pupils to be found. At a recent national election the turnout at the polls in the south was tiny, and locals were apparently punished by the Taleban for voting. The peasant farmers disliked terrorism and the ways of the Taleban but understood their religious fundamentalism, and they were cautious about the unknown and strange ways of the West.

Two days after our arrival we flew north-west to Bamiyan, 'the valley of the Buddhas', home of the Hazara tribe with their wider faces and almond eyes. Our tiny twenty-seater aircraft swooped through the stunning mountains, snow still in the creases of the brown earth spread out below, green river valleys patterned irregularly with small fields lined with eucalypts. It is the closest I have been to the view that a serious climber must have as he reaches the top of the world. We came down on a brushed earthen runway surrounded by awesome peaks, pale brown everywhere. Their timelessness and the enormity of this world sat incongruously alongside my own recent grief. These mountains and this country had been here for a long time, unchanged, part of a universal peace. Mark's was one small death, almost irrelevant, yet for me it was everything.

We arrived in Bamiyan after days of flooding and wondered if we could find a hotel, if we were to sleep at all. After waiting several hours for the waters to subside we finally drove our 4x4 through a swollen river to the hotel, unsure if our vehicle would stay upright in the torrent. The hotel was quite deserted, managed by one man, and some rooms were unserviced and smelly because of the impossibility of working on religious days: the women did the cooking, cleaning, and serving.

The huge Buddhas had been carved into the cliff face between the fourth and sixth centuries, and then bombed by the Taleban in March 2001 into nothing, apparently in a frenzy of religious idealism and hatred of idolatry. Now there were just the massive shells of the caves around them, a menacing presence watching over the valley.

Around us we could see the positive effects of the Western invasion, spring shoots and change. Here people were friendlier, smiling at us because of international aid and funding for project work. There had been peace here for ten years, since the area had been taken from the Taleban by the Americans in November 2001. There had always been local hatred of the southern Pashtun tribes, and so the attempted control by Pashtun Taleban had been relatively easy to defeat. Nowadays Taleban are imprisoned here, they are the enemy.

The day that the rest of the party were to go on a day tour to local lakes, I asked instead for a guide to take me down to the local bazaar. He was a lean-limbed, agile and thoughtful young man, speaking fair English he had learned as a tourist guide. As Mark would also have done, he insisted that I jump across frightening swollen rivulets criss-crossing the road, still almost impassable with the rains. His young energy seemed not to understand my age. We talked for hours as we strolled from the hotel to the village and around the bazaar. One could buy beautiful hand-crafted silver and ceramics inlaid with locally mined lapis lazuli, fabrics and carpets. Curiously, most of the foodstuffs in the village were from Pakistan, the closest neighbour; these trade connections are strong even in this remote part of north-west Afghanistan.

My guide wanted the best for himself: educational opportunity, work. As we walked along we saw children coming out of school, the girls in black tunics and white scarves. The local governor was an educated woman, and all have free education, but that was only in this part of Afghanistan. He said that here they are nationalistic and care about Afghanistan, and that Western influence has persuaded them that tribal differences are less important than national interests. Nevertheless, the old tribal hatreds seemed to be there, powerful, and he said he would fight a Taleb if one came here.

The next day we walked in the wonderful rocky copper-pink mountains with their drifts of white sediment, home at present only to a few goats herded by women, and gliding, soaring hawks. Our guide there said that tribal differences would stop any mining of the mineral wealth in these peaks.

These peasant people appeared to be important here, the pawns, rooks and even knights and bishops of this world, an old mosaic. The mountains seemed to define their fundamental values, and the people farming the rich little valleys have learned over time to live with their threat, building high walls around their family compounds, welcoming only fellow tribesmen, distrusting strangers and visitors. Tribal elders, mullahs and warlords have had to lead aggressively to provide protection, to be dedicated and authoritarian in order to deal with this fierce country and its intruders. These leaders were to be obeyed since there were few police, only a limited national judicial system. I was told that the people have learned not to think ahead; they cannot be sure of what comes, what work and safety there will be in the future. Allah, one's tribe and one's own family will provide. I could see that this was not the world of the West.

The young guide at the hotel became my companion for a few days whilst the group travelled; she and I were by ourselves. She was a Hazara girl of about twenty, educated, intelligent and ambitious, wanting to travel and study abroad, and she was friendly and happy to talk for a few days.

She told me about life here, parts of it frustrating to her. She said change was just on the surface, local people say what Westerners want to hear, but behind closed doors the old values dictate. Even here in this 'progressive' outpost she described a male and macho world, one in which the gentler and adorning influences of women are hidden behind the high walls. Usually only the men work, often supporting large families, they are stronger and so more able to deal with the harsh survival of this world. Women need their husbands' permission to work and the women's jobs are usually menial, cleaning or working in the fields. Many pleasures are disapproved of that get in the way of work.

Loveless arranged marriages are set up for financial gain and families are ashamed if their daughters choose not to marry. Sisters' dowries allow their brothers to pay for better wives, and so if daughters want more independence for themselves, whole families suffer. Marriage is kept within the tribe to those known and safe. Wives give birth to between six and twelve children, who are nurtured until the age of three and then left to roam the streets locally. The women become lazy, given little responsibility; they seemed self-effacing, under-confident. Their comfort is family, other women and talk. If men bully and are violent to their wives, the wives have little recourse. My friend told me that contraception was previously unheard of, condoms only recently introduced, and many women die in childbirth. Kissing is a new pleasure, first seen in American movies, and the delights of the naked body are forbidden, sexual intercourse often fully clothed.

Islam is there to comfort, make order of death and unhappiness, and give precious quiet time to reflect in a life where work and survival are so intertwined.

On the day we left Bamiyan my friend appeared after

breakfast, weeping and upset. Seven Western aid workers who were close friends of hers from Kabul had been murdered in a relatively safe country area some distance away. They were victims now, and the unfairness of it cut deep into her youthful idealism and sense of justice. They had been shot and their valuables and identity documents stolen, perhaps by simple thieves. But the Taleban had claimed responsibility, a warning to other intrepid Westerners who might want to come to help. It was said that they were Christian Aid workers and carried Bibles.

Everywhere one could see that being un-Islamic is disapproved of, along with Christianity, the Bible and the cross. Christianity is punished nationally with a jail sentence. Right-wing Islamic fundamentalists have been blamed in the West for this current Afghan conflict, but when one sees such an intense dislike of Christianity, one has to wonder how much of the conflict could in fact be a religious war waged by young men for whom fighting is the way. In country areas, those who do not follow the Prophet are considered unclean, and if entertained in traditional households have to eat from separate plates, and afterwards all traces carefully wiped away. One could see the roots of such old customs: once-sensible rules in tribal valleys when illness is brought by strangers and carries such a price.

As I became more aware, so Mark's diary and letters had more meaning, more immediacy. I was beginning to see how it must have been for the platoon as they tried to negotiate with the locals, explain themselves, live in the country.

Back to Kabul, and then we drove through the Panshir valley to a monument being built to house the tomb of Massoud, the great Tajic (northern) resistance fighter who was killed only days before 9/11. I watched as a family arrived for lunch at a beautiful elegant Muslim shrine in the valley. The family got a lamb out of the boot of the battered car, the children dancing around, excited by a day out. I was touched that they had brought the family lamb with them, but I was naïve. I watched horrified as they cut its throat in front of us, a feast for a picnic.

The harsh stony treeless mountains around us were washed pale with Turner colours, pink, brown, orange; they were omnipresent, the source of precious rains and rivers, and for centuries a safe haven for marauders and infidels. Now perhaps they hide Taleban and Al Qaeda. They were littered with mines and along the mountain passes we saw the occasional menacing wrecks of abandoned Russian tanks. Here were the lessons of history, black and rusty in the mountains, and above the thin still blue sky, innocent for now in August but soon to change.

Still mourning myself, I was curious about how these people dealt with the death of their own. Did their religion, their lifestyle, make these deaths any different to those in the West? Norine introduced me to Aziz, who had lost a brother to the Taleban and who happened to be working in her charity's London office. He came to talk to me some days after I had returned home.

Aziz was twenty-six, a handsome Afghan keen to embrace life in a modern international way, but still a Pashtun, brought up and educated in Kabul. He was a child of the wars, but a Muslim who was beginning to question the destruction he saw around him. He was the eldest of eleven children, with seven sisters and now only two brothers, and he had worked now for many years with the Western Allies, helping provide for his parents and siblings. His father was a property developer in Kabul, his mother stayed at home. Some of his uncles lived abroad, having fled the troubles. However, the generation earlier, his great-uncles, disapproved of this family contact and cooperation with the West and Western forces – they said it was shameful and lacked propriety. Aziz wanted to choose his own wife but his father had once arranged a marriage for him: the young man was so angry he had not gone home for many months, if only to avoid the situation.

Aziz's brother had been very close to him; they had shared a bed, a room and a childhood, playing and talking together, dreaming of how they would be as they grew up. His brother became an interpreter with the American troops, and was killed by a Taleban roadside bomb in 2008. Aziz was told only recently about his brother's death, till then believing him to be out and about, working and travelling. He was still tearful, unable to believe that his brother was gone. He said his mother was still distraught, visiting the grave daily, for a while losing interest and 'too sad to wear shoes'. His father was tight-lipped, insisting on looking ahead. Aziz said he often went to the place where he had last spoken to his brother in London to cry, to relive memories – it was in a side alley between the Afghan embassy and a church. He was still trying to hold onto his brother with mementoes of him, making a wall box of his medals and bits of his life. His anguish was palpable as he tried to understand, and there was a sense that for him Islam did not give enough answers. I understood completely how he felt.

Aziz had spent much time in the unhappy southern provinces, and thought that it would be difficult to build up a national police force and army in just a few years. The situation was complex, but he felt unable to contemplate the awfulness of an Afghanistan in a few years when the Americans left. He described the Taleban wanting to return to medieval ways, ruling with terror, people fearful of their brutality. I was aware that his own position must be dangerous there, and indeed he thought he should leave, although he clearly wanted to stay.

Thus I had seen something of the country over nine days; I had talked to locals when I could and tried to understand. Later I realised how important the trip had been to me: it gave me a local context for what I knew about the Army, the war and, in the end, Mark's death.

It was a remarkable trip, the stuff of thought for months to come.

What was I left with? In Kabul it had been easy to see the potential benefits that Western forces and international aid could bring. But change in this country has been very slow, and I could see that these people were clearly struggling now with enforced nationalism, a far cry from internationalism. In a very short period of time the Allies wanted security, a national police force and an army, as well as democracy, education for all and equal rights for women. These things have taken centuries to develop in the West and it is easy to see the difficulties with them happening here. Perhaps electronics, televisions, mobiles phones, computers and finally tourism and travel may change these old ways, just as new knowledge of the trade winds in 1492 changed the local world and all that time ago internationalism was slowly born. But despite other wars, other campaigns, this country remains relatively untouched by the West and its influences, unlike many other Muslim countries. Democracy felt a long way off.

Those bare soaring mountains remained the most powerful symbol of the country for me, the landscape an unrepentant dictator of how a people should be. I was there in summer, but winter must be brutal. Mark had been injured in a compound on the plains of Helmand, yet I saw the same family compounds everywhere, tiny high-walled windowless family and tribal units locked into survival, not curious about the West and other ways of doing things. These are old ways and old pressures, the pressures of nature, geography and a religion that tells these people how to live and have hope. Infidels and insurgents had caused social systems to tighten up over many centuries; violence should be paid back with violence. Old ways of justice, an eye for an eye. One could only hope that a universal need for peace, a dislike of brutality and inequality, a need to live and protect one's own peacefully, will win out and that one day other ways will be chosen by all.

But fighting and guns have always been the currency of survival here. There are young men with time, idealism and energy to enjoy the world of guns and machines, fighting and winning, and who are paid to do it. Revenge has been a necessary and powerful weapon when marauders and other tribes do not have to obey local laws; it is part of the culture here, often continuing for generations. I was reminded of Mark's comment that some of his Afghan soldiers chose to fight with Western forces in order to avenge the deaths of relatives by the Taleban: and of the proverb that 'a Pashtun can wait his entire life for his revenge and then curse himself for his impatience', mentioned in a speech by General David Petraeus, Commander of the US forces in Afghanistan in 2010.

I had been told of the civilian death rate in Helmand since the beginning of the conflict in 2011. Between

2007 and 2011, 12,793 civilians had been killed, 66.9 per cent by the Taleban, the rest by pro-government forces. I could see how anti-Western flames might continue to smoulder, if not burn brightly. I was reminded that one reason given for the lateness of the helicopter for Mark was that it had been sent off to pick up an injured local, presumably because the Army worried about the consequences of that injury. Western commanders could use 'courageous restraint' and discourage or almost forbid the killing of locals. But Mark had told me how civilians, often children with mobile phones, report the movements of soldiers on a regular basis, and the soldiers can do little to stop them.

Whilst I saw the anger here, I could also understand the fear of terrorism in the West, the sense of impotence in the face of violent radicalised hatred. Initially charged with winning a 'war' against an idea, the Army is there to establish some national security, partly so that safety in the UK is not compromised. A stable government speaking for the people of course will help withstand the buffeting of political forces in that part of the world. But what of the old controls, the old stabilising forces, the old ways? I could see that President Karzai must have to balance intense tribal pressures and traditions, bartering power and using money apparently corruptly, as well as dealing with the pressure from the West. These very expensive short-term solutions were perhaps building problems for the future.

By 2009 the war was no longer called a counter-terrorist conflict since it was unclear whether Al Qaeda was still an influence there; it was now called 'counter-insurgency'. Its emphasis was now on defeating those young angry insurgents (who may perhaps be Taleban but not necessarily) and winning the hearts and minds of the local people. But I could see that when the Western powers arrive and sing from a different religious, social and ethical hymn sheet, 'winning hearts and minds' cannot be easy. British soldiers are there just for six months and they have a job to do, they have little time to build up relationships.

One had to wonder why those British generals chose the deeply conservative southern Helmand as their area of battle in 2006, whilst other NATO countries avoided it. It was a statement about the confidence of the British Army then, but it now seemed misplaced. There must have been insufficient knowledge at intelligence, political and tactical levels of what was in store, not anticipating an insurgency and guerrilla war. Did they know the Taleban and how they would fight, with IEDs, snipers and deception? Did they plan to develop the military resource for such a situation, despite the lack of vehicles, helicopters and men seen there since?

There are clearly lessons to be learned. When I met General Sir Nick Parker, previously ISAF Deputy Commander, he said openly that at the time that Mark died the situation was indeed far too difficult, equipment and many more soldiers were needed. It was a war very slow in its winning, if it was being won at all.

I was reminded of the outcome of the first Anglo-Afghan war in 1842, and the evocative painting *The Remnants of an Army* (1879) by Lady Elizabeth Butler, showing William Bryden, the only officer of a garrison of 16,500 to survive the retreat from Kabul.

This had been only the first of many campaigns, all ending in tragedy and rout.

Months later, in November 2010, I watched a BBC news item about Nad-e-Ali, close to where Mark had been based. It described how an unsettled peace had been brought to that small area after the arrival of approximately 6,000 US troops, eighteen months of military effort and many deaths. It was a tiny area, and at what cost had a temporary calm been won, with us soon to withdraw?

I was here with Mark. I could only hope that his death could have some value, some meaning.

CHAPTER 10

FINAL

Now it is all over, the seasons have come and gone and time very slowly passed, what am I left with?

I expected that with Mark's death I would feel guilt and anger, as there always is with death. I feel some guilt, but he had a good life and was very loved, and it passes easily. Perhaps inevitably, I feel anger – with the Coroner's process, with parts of the MOD and, finally, with war. I have tried to tame that anger and put it where it can reasonably and fairly be put. But I am reminded of the rage and condemnation of the First World War poets after they had been on the front line, and of the lines of Wilfred Owen's poem, 'Dulce et Decorum Est':

Bent double, like old beggars under sacks,
Knock-kneed, coughing like hags, we cursed through sludge,
Till on the haunting flares we turned our backs
And towards our distant rest began to trudge.
Men marched asleep. Many had lost their boots
But limped on, blood-shod. All went lame; all blind;
Drunk with fatigue; deaf even to the hoots

Of tired, outstripped Five-Nines that dropped behind.

GAS! Gas! Quick, boys! – An ecstasy of fumbling,
Fitting the clumsy helmets just in time;
But someone still was yelling out and stumbling,
And flound'ring like a man in fire or lime …
Dim, through the misty panes and thick green light,
As under a green sea, I saw him drowning.

In all my dreams, before my helpless sight,
He plunges at me, guttering, choking, drowning.

If in some smothering dreams you too could pace
Behind the wagon that we flung him in,
And watch the white eyes writhing in his face,
His hanging face, like a devil's sick of sin;
If you could hear, at every jolt, the blood
Come gargling from the froth-corrupted lungs,
Obscene as cancer, bitter as the cud
Of vile, incurable sores on innocent tongues,
My friend, you would not tell with such high zest
To children ardent for some desperate glory,
The old Lie; *Dulce et decorum est*
Pro patria mori.

Mark died as a soldier, and these poets remind us of the
horror of war death, perhaps almost forgotten in modern
times but understood so powerfully and poignantly by

234

those older. Mark is buried in a peaceful manicured war cemetery, but the beauty and glory of that place and the ceremony of his funeral have never masked for me the horror of his death, the horror of war.

Those First World War poets, the art and the postcards of the time, remind us of the universal distress of the death of a son, a young person, a soldier. The fundamental Christian image repeats itself over and over in thousands of war memorials in the Western world: a limp, dead, elegant Christ, symbol of the best of mankind morally and perhaps physically, with an anguished mother and adoring, confused and leaderless disciples. That 'ultimate sacrifice' is interpreted by Christianity as a symbol of love, but those are also the words of war.

I have heard it said that withdrawal from Afghanistan would be difficult for the families of the dead, as their loss would seem to have achieved little. The Prime Minister reassured us in a television interview on 5 October 2010 that Mark's death was 'not for nothing, it was to help Afghans secure their own country', thus acknowledging that death and sacrifice should have a purpose, something achieved. I too wanted Mark's death not to have been in vain, for it to have been useful in some way, and perhaps seeing positive and lasting changes in Afghanistan would help.

As a civilian, I carried with me other feelings about death, only partly related to those Army ideas of 'duty'. Some part of me believes, as Islam does, that we owe something for being alive, that we have a duty to repay that debt, that we need to be good people to help fulfil our obligation for being here at all. An early death curtails that repayment, there is not enough time, youth is just a playful selfish preparation before the heavier demands of life. Is it possible to fulfil that obligation in a 'good cause'?

After Mark's death, the many letters written to me implied past loss, and I knew that many understood my pain. These letters explained something that has taken me a long time to understand.

16/07/09

Dear Mrs Evison,

I just wanted to write a few times to offer you my condolences … Your son, Mark, was attempting to do something which he knew was difficult and dangerous and yet he had the leadership skills, courage and determination to do his very best, despite the risk.

I do believe in the saying: 'To live in the hearts of those we love is not to die.'

Words of sympathy are rather inadequate, I fear.

I enclose a small donation for your foundation and wish I could afford more.

With my best wishes,

CC

14/07/09

…There are no words in my vocabulary; today's *Telegraph* said it all, and tonight I will read it all to my ten-year-old son, so that we can appreciate what it is to live in a country of political and religious freedom.

But for Mark's mother, father, and sister please know that foremost our thoughts and prayers are with them, and when we think of what is fine, what is good, and what is love, we shall think of Mark. May his soul rest in peace,

Truly Yours,

N, A, R and R

Most who wrote were just able to admire Mark for his actions, the fact that he had lived and died lovingly made him admirable. Just doing his best, fulfilling his obligations to his men was enough. His was a heroic life, an inspiration to others to be selfless, and by this alone his living would not be in vain. His life had found in its very end its own intrinsic worth. His final action was a noble action, to be applauded, dying because he loved his men enough to want to save them and sacrifice himself. I could see that one should be proud of his conduct, although I remain resentful and unconvinced about the circumstances of his death, and as a mother I feel that there is almost no circumstance that could 'justify' a son's loss.

Humans have always made sacrifices, giving our best for the good of the majority. It is a powerful idea in all cultures. It may be because at some level we are essentially magical, superstitious and symbolic animals, and for thousands of years through different beliefs and faiths we have felt a need to placate unknown spiritual forces with sacrifice. The Army is an old institution that has come to understand the importance of pomp and pageantry, of morale and obedience, and of rituals for dealing with death. Its chosen path has been to see it as a necessary sacrifice and teach its soldiers that this is so, which perhaps it is for fighting men, and to glorify it. On the Cenotaph is written, 'To our glorious dead.'

At RMA Sandhurst young recruits are now asked to read Mark's diary, to think about his example of 'selfless commitment', his 'ultimate sacrifice', and then to visit his grave at Brookwood. They need to understand that they have to be prepared, in one second, to do the same, to give their young lives. To these recruits, his death implies not only duty, dying so that others may live, but also love, love for one's mates, perhaps even love for one's country. This institutional and national acceptance of fighting and heroic sacrifice is spoken for by the flags of hundreds of years of campaigns proudly erect around the Guards Chapel where Mark's funeral was held. Over many centuries it has become the glorification of war and war death.

Happily our view of death in battle has changed over the years. Throwing soldiers at one another across lines and shooting deserters as in the First World War is not acceptable now. People are less likely to draw comfort from religious belief; they see a modern world working so hard to protect life, and they see less death at an early age than ever before. Thus, young death is more of a shock, and perhaps people care more. They want to look after their young men, not offer them for sacrifice in this conflict. People clearly hope that wars can be fought more sensibly than in the past, that the excesses of human desecration seen in both world wars and still in living memory, can be avoided. The awareness of those traumatic experiences and advances in medical technology have reminded us that human life is precious, all human life, even to the first point of biological union. No longer are the excesses of warmongering acceptable and pointless deaths condoned – a major poll in 2011 gave human loss as the main reason for opposing the war. Science has revealed life's magic, and this magic is to be admired, revered and preserved.

Importantly, the repatriation rituals seen on the streets of Wootton Bassett in Wiltshire caught the nation's imagination – a fuse has been lit as public support for wounded and dead soldiers and their families has surged, a national homage. The bodies have been brought back as a final gesture of respect, to allow them to be given to their mourning families. But that has also had a profound effect on the nation's awareness of this war, perhaps a modern equivalent to earlier war poems. The MOD has now moved its repatriations back to Brize Norton in Oxfordshire, but the effect of Wootten Bassett seems to have been profound.

One of course needs an army to defend a nation, one trained and hopefully equipped to do its job. Young men have always enjoyed the adrenalin of fighting, war and destruction, the assertion of their manhood, their supremacy and autonomy, being warriors. In Britain this young human thrust and energy finds its outlet in the Armed Forces, where it coincides with institutional and national interest. Politicians are responsible for the care with which the Army is deployed, and in the end they are responsible for the care of the soldiers within it. You fight for us and we will look after you – that should be the institutional standard. If we ask them to fight and die for us, we should keep our side of the bargain. Soldiers should be protected, properly equipped to do the job we have asked them to do so that they are less likely to lose their lives or suffer debilitating injury; the Military Covenant should be integral to that, as the soldiers expect.

In my opinion, our politicians have wanted a solution and power on the cheap, paying as little as possible for it. Our soldiers have not had what they have needed to be effective, despite the huge industry behind them. Mark's story highlights this. Resources – helicopters, radio equipment, medical equipment – were, and possibly still are, short. If these men's lives are at risk, if radios are inadequate and helicopters are not available, surely expensive pieces of kit elsewhere should be done without instead and human lives put first. MOD 'hardware', ships and planes, come to mind. Sensible decisions should be made to ensure there are working radios for the men (if these are 'more important than guns') and fast access to medical help if soldiers get hurt.

Young men want to fight; the public understands the need for sacrifice; and there are politicians who want to wage wars for power. But there is also a huge military and industrial complex set up around the 'business' of war – jobs and economies – which is a powerful pressure to fight.

President D. Eisenhower, an old soldier, said in a speech three days before he left office:

> Our military organization today bears little relation to that known by any of my predecessors in peacetime, or indeed by the fighting men of World War II or Korea.
>
> …This conjunction of an immense military establishment and a large arms industry is new in the American experience. The total influence – economic, political, even spiritual – is felt in every city, every State house, every office of the Federal government. We recognize the imperative need for this development. Yet we must not fail to comprehend its grave implications. Our toil, resources and livelihood are all involved; so is the very structure of our society.
>
> In the councils of government, we must guard against the acquisition of unwarranted influence, whether sought or unsought, by the military industrial complex. The potential for the disastrous rise of misplaced power exists and will persist.
>
> We must never let the weight of this combination

endanger our liberties or democratic processes. We should take nothing for granted. Only an alert and knowledgeable citizenry can compel the proper meshing of the huge industrial and military machinery of defense with our peaceful methods and goals, so that security and liberty may prosper together.

Military-Industrial Complex Speech, Dwight D. Eisenhower, 1961: Public Papers of the Presidents, Dwight D. Eisenhower, 1960, pp. 1035–40

Because of these pressures, conflicts need a strong morality to them to prevent war- and power-mongering for political gain, for greed, for power. Clearly a defensive war has an easy morality, its roots solid in self-protection, but the voting public has to carefully monitor the reasons for other wars.

The present Afghanistan conflict had its roots in the dead of 9/11, an act of terrorism which killed almost 3,000 innocents in horrific circumstances and struck a fundamental blow to American values, freedoms, lifestyle and politics. The invasion was initially explained by politicians as a defensive war against terrorism, the saving of innocent people from its brutality and unpredictability. It was accepted by the public as such, although there was perhaps an unpleasant hint of American retribution in the response.

But the aims of the conflict are now counter-insurgency rather than counter-terrorism, its morality is less obvious, and it has become essentially a political conflict, one in which over 2,000 US troops had been killed by 2012. One could argue that a political war should continue to press hard for more political solutions – war is destructive and we have Iraq nearby, a painful memory. Afghanistan needs building, not destroying, and we are there now trying to rebuild as well as to fight. One hears recent accounts of improvement in some areas, some seeds of stability, a trained local army, but this culture is old. When the West pulls out will there be sufficient change to alter the old tribal blood feud culture, particularly in country areas, or will the predictions of civil war be realised? Without understanding the people well, that culture, do we not lay ourselves open to covertly and unknowingly encouraging the abuse of Western money, power and influence? We remember this in the very near past, with the early US encouragement of the Taleban in an effort to stabilise an unsettled Afghanistan after the failed Russian invasion. Arguably we need to understand such cultures better before we fight these new wars.

Mark's death highlighted important issues to do with the Army. At a high strategic level the British Army seems to have attempted to punch above its weight in taking on Helmand. Many problems became apparent: short circuits in the chain of information, command, responsibility and accountability across the organisation.

A big organisation loses a relationship with truth across its many layers, but in the case of the MOD and

Army, rank and status drive another wedge through effective communication. Communication appears to have been a major hurdle, and it would appear that senior officers could not explain and ask strongly and clearly enough for more. Just as soldiers are not allowed to speak out, perhaps these officers found it difficult to ask, bound by years of discouragement or perhaps even the effect on promotion. It may be that the Army structure and ethos from the top down does not encourage listening, hearing and paying attention to the ordinary soldiers on the ground: ordinary soldiers find it difficult to explain to their senior officers, obedience is all. The lower ranks have no real voice upwards and across to the parent organisation.

There is an Army attitude that war has always been untidy, difficult and fought with shortages, and this view arguably has not served the Army's needs well, both when asking for more resources and funding, and also when dealing with very poor procurement and supply chains. A letter dated 18 May 2009 by the senior air commodore K. L. O'Dea at Command Headquarters Joint Forces, written with reference to the circumstances of Mark's death and Major Bettison's Learning Account, states that 'A Service Inquiry would add little to the LA [Learning Account], and it is recommended that a waiver is granted.' The incident and the death of this talented officer was just passed by internally with only the minor local operational changes recommended by the Learning

Account. Why? Was it assumed to be bad luck, was there nothing to be learned?

The situation Mark and the platoon found themselves in was just not sensible. The muddle over Mark's death seemed to reflect a more fundamental Army and political muddle over Afghanistan, as well as a muddle about itself. One has to admire the efforts of all on the ground to do their best in the situation that Mark was in, and the hospital diary bears witness to this: one senses the great pressure, fear, heat and enemy fire, the hostile environment. But if one looks at the much broader picture, whatever the reason, the campaign may not be judged kindly by history.

Mark's death highlighted how the legal department of the MOD handles Coroner's inquests and the families of lost soldiers. It was easy to be angry when facing uncaring legal bureaucrats doing a job intuitively brutish. The MOD is always defensive, controlling information in the interests of national security but also, I increasingly felt, in this particular situation in the interest of the institution and its own self-preservation. The result was not a credit to it. The MOD customarily 'named and blamed' if they could, as I had seen in other recent inquests, so in the absence of that it was easy to assume there was systemic fault which they would not acknowledge. Mark and other serving men deserved better. If mistakes have been made there should be some internal and public accountability so that the public understand and are satisfied. This aspect of the MOD's response at both a personal and strategic level felt dated, archaic even, and unduly insensitive.

In Mark's complex case, the Coroner's inquest was arguably not the right process for considering his death. There should have been a full inquiry for the benefit of others, from the time of the shooting or even before, with the power to investigate other areas as well. It should have been tasked to look at the issues of communications, helicopter availability, the 'golden hour' and shortages in medical kit – all contributing to Mark's death, and so with the question of why Mark died at its heart. Family, friends and the general public wanted to know and had a right to know, and the MOD may have benefited from an independent look at what happened. Mark's death was perhaps preventable, and for that reason it needed proper examination which it could not get in a busy Coroner's court.

As well as the impact of Mark's death at a more public and even national level, there are those at home, the wide circle who loved him. The death of all soldiers affects not only families but whole communities.

For me personally, now I also understand the pain of the loss of someone so young. Mark's death will always be a scar on my life, the taking away of a precious child. For me the pain of love feels deeper than physical pain, that endless sad place always there. I would not have believed that the pain of a child's death could be so wracking, so complete. It is the breaking up of intense biological bonds built to nurture and endure, it is a shattering of what was intended. One knows of nature's anger with the unnatural splitting of an atom: so a parent feels a child's death.

Since his death, Mark is always there but not there, a memory that cannot go away. He is never far from my mind, and in the dark of the night and in the mornings he almost returns. I am reminded sometimes of what the Christian resurrection means, the symbolic journey of that very loved person many centuries ago into the ether of souls, to be there to judge us. In the same way I like to think I still have Mark nearby, aware of it all. Perhaps that is why that strange Christian message is so easily understood by so many, why it makes sense, why it represents hope. Death is at the root of Christianity and perhaps all religion.

For Mark's sister Elizabeth there is her loss of a play-mate, companion and friend of twenty-six years, and the future loss of the fundamental support of a brother over a lifetime, an uncle for her children. It is a great lifelong loss for her. Always very precious to me, she is now an only child.

To his friends, those who grew up with him, shared dreams and hopes with him, played with him and loved him, his death feels inexplicable and hard to reconcile. Who can take his place? What can one do with the memories? They are too young to deal with this loss.

Aziz, the young Afghan who has lost his brother, underlined for me the pain to all who have lost someone.

I have become aware of the intense sadness of Mark's soldiers over his death, the pain and powerlessness of watching a bonded and loved comrade and friend die. They never forget, it leaves them with deep traces often for a lifetime. Perhaps for them it may serve to underline the magic of life and of being alive, the appreciation of what life means in themselves and those they care about.

For Mark himself there must have been that under-standing, as he bled whilst still conscious, that it might all be over. At twenty-six, the rest of one's life is a lot to give away. He had written on 30 April 2009, less than two weeks before his death: 'Life is fragile and out here it feels like it can be removed in an instant. It almost makes life even more valuable and shows the fragility that many in the West I believe do not understand.' Did he understand the significance of what he wrote about life, its painful detritus? As he lay there injured and in pain waiting for a helicopter, he said that he did not want to die. He had been at Sandhurst and talked about death, but now it was here. Those fighting, seeing injury and death all around, understand more than the civil servants and politicians in Whitehall. Many planning this war in the MOD will have seen very little active service, and possibly not in a conflict so tough.

This was a personal journey, a personal book. I know that many others have made such a journey, some have lost sons, and I watch new widows struggling alone with their frustrated love and the needs and upset of their fatherless children. But this has been my own. It began with the end of Mark's, and that has changed me and others for ever. But it has made me very aware of the magic of other people who understand, the kindness of others who can imagine, and also the sometimes stony face and heart of institutions.

One light through all has been the Mark Evison Foundation, set up immediately after his death, and the good will, interest, enthusiasm and idealism it has engendered. It is a lasting legacy to Mark.

In his twenty-six years Mark lit up many other lives because of how he was. He died a loving, dutiful and heroic death caring for his men, but at great personal cost. Perhaps the last words are those of Tolstoy, who fought and then turned against war: 'Where love is there God is also'.

AFTERWORD: THE MARK
EVISON FOUNDATION

The Mark Evison Foundation has been the silver lining. Its seeds were planted during our few days in Selly Oak Hospital, as I saw those young people saying goodbye to their friend, their brother, lying before them limp and unresponsive. Later, I was talking with a friend about some kind of memorial to Mark and he suggested a charitable trust (which the friend was then very generous in supporting). It was something practical we could do as a conduit for some of our energy, but also for our almost impossible regret. The Foundation was born at speed during a time of great sadness, a time when it felt easier in some ways to get on and do rather than stand still and let grief overwhelm us.

By the day of the funeral, less than three weeks later, the Foundation had a name, a charity number, an agreed purpose, all with the help of generous lawyers – and a bank account. Its beneficiaries were to be young people, and its purpose their physical, mental and personal development. That was Mark, his fascination, what he had so loved about Sandhurst.

The following letters were written to me after the publication of Mark's diary on 12 July in the *Daily Telegraph*:

To the Mark Evison Foundation,

£200 sent to you in admiration after reading the excellent article about the brave young Mark and his grieving mother.

From two elderly (childless) friends in a nursing home in Blandford, Dorset.

L and V

I think the article has aroused a lot of interest.

23/07/09

Dear Mrs Evison,

I enclose a cheque for £50 to go towards the Mark Evison Foundation.

I was so moved by his diary and your article in the *Telegraph* (this is being written with watery eyes). What a wonderful young man, what a talent with words. Your loss and everyone around him must be unbearable.

His life is no longer one of those grim statistics we hear on the news. It is difficult to comprehend the pain of yours and other families.

I hope the Mark Evison Foundation brings some magic to other people's lives and Mark's spirit will live on.

With best wishes,

B

These letters caught our mood exactly.

We wanted the Foundation to reflect Mark's unusual capacity to be life-enhancer. That became its strap line: 'Bring out the best in you.' We would use the funds raised and donated to encourage, help, motivate, to make young people feel strengthened, to begin to develop leadership qualities. It would allow young people to develop their potential, to show initiative, to take calculated risks and so increase confidence, and to nurture a can-do attitude when financial constraints dampen it. It was to represent a brighter, caring, supporting and developing side of life, the side that Mark had been to others. We wanted to give non-academic awards to those who tried as Mark had always done, right to the end as he fought not to give up despite his wounds. It was the perfect memorial, our memorial to him.

The Foundation has been run so far with the help of Mark's friends, young people helping other young people. Many have devoted much time to it, and even more have donated, at the funeral and after, happy that it would be used well. Since its inception, the Foundation has brought out the best in most involved with it, although its path as been difficult and demanding at times. When we first set it up we were babes in arms, untutored in how we should do things. The trustees were initially three of Mark's friends and his sister, but as the Foundation expands, more experienced trustees will be invited to join the board. It has given great joy and attracted great interest, including considerable media attention; receptions have been held at 10 Downing Street, 11 Downing Street and Prince Charles's garden at Highgrove. It has been operated largely by volunteers, and several generous and understanding individuals have offered their time and, on occasions, wonderful auction prizes. This support has been touching by any standards – and it has allowed us to grow.

Making young people and schools aware of the awards and how the process works takes time and is an ongoing challenge. For our first-ever award, fellow trustee Sholto and I interviewed two young lads of sixteen and seventeen years, Luke and Tomos, from Dulwich College, who wanted to climb the four highest UK peaks in four days using only public transport with their dog Anvil. They did it with two hours to spare. They were inspiring with their energy, enthusiasm, innocence and flair. They made a very touching video about their trip, then shown to the many other interested young people. This was the first time we saw how Mark's story was a clear catalyst for these young men, with energy and a yearning for independence and to test themselves.

Our second award went to dBand: four teenage musicians who used the funds for a recording studio session. Their aim was to put their songs on iTunes, with all proceeds to go to the Foundation. This is their story:

After we received the generous award from the Mark Evison Foundation in June 2010, we were able to begin putting our plans into action. We started by getting together as a band and created a group of initial songs. We spent plenty of time developing these songs, discarding a few and changing some beyond recognition. We set ourselves the target of having three songs ready by October, so that we could book the recording studio for our winter half term.

Following the summer holidays we booked a recording slot at Garage Studios, a recording studio run by Martin Smith in East Grinstead. We spent three long days in the studio, managing to record three of our songs. These three days turned out to be a wonderful experience, having the chance to work with a fantastic music producer and experiencing the satisfaction of seeing the songs we had created become recorded tracks.

The foundation gave us fantastic support and the opportunity to spend time in a recording studio. However, more than this the award has really motivated us to keep working hard at developing our band into the future taking it beyond merely a pastime at school to becoming a longer-lasting project. Spending time in the studio represents a stage in our development and we plan to continue writing new songs in the future.

Thus we gave our first memorial awards in Mark's two secondary schools, cutting our teeth on new ideas and processes with the support of those schools. In early 2011 we decided to take the awards to non-fee paying schools, initially, at least, in the London region. I have told Mark's story and shown the boys' video to large sixth form classes at these schools, and I have admired the teachers attempting to motivate, instil a value system and encourage effort, all underpinned by their belief in discipline and hope. I see how Mark's story and how he was can inspire these young people, when their lives are often local and without such positive role models, when sometimes home situations work against support and hope.

Later that year, Faruk and Brandon from Mossbourne Community School in Hackney won an award for a five-day cycling challenge to France. I met them when they had just returned, and what a thrill it had been for them. Faruk had never been abroad before, and Brandon only to France once when he stayed with relatives, hardly going out. They said how important it was to them that they were able to choose what they wanted to do for their own challenge, and when they returned they wrote the following:

During a whole year assembly Mrs Margaret Evison came in and talked to us about her organisation including how it began and what they do. Mrs Evison told us about her late son Mark Evison; how brave he was, how he liked to challenge himself and how competitive he was, which was truly inspiring and inspired me to challenge myself and do something outside the norm. After hearing what some of the other winners of the Mark

Evison Challenge had done I went back and had a word with a few teachers and external sources; I then began drafting ideas.

Coming from a community that lacks opportunities, winning the Mark Evison Award enabled me to realise a dream. Having studied French at GCSE and becoming interested in the French culture I came up with an idea: 'The Commune Challenge', that also combined my love of cycling. A friend, Brandon Oyungunga, and I planned to do a bike ride where we cycled to twenty-five different communes (each commune roughly equal to the size of a borough) covering over 130 km in the space of three days. I presented my idea to the foundation and won the award.

The challenge was a test both physically and mentally. There were times, in the heat of the French summer and after hours of cycling, that Brandon I and felt like quitting, but through teamwork and determination we managed to complete it. Through doing the challenge I have learnt so much and had a major boost in self-belief and confidence. I planned the whole thing myself and I now know how to go about turning visions into reality. Being only seventeen, I got a real feel of independence as there was no one in France to look out for us or give us any extra money. We had to be careful with money and good at time-keeping to make sure that we were on schedule during our ride and had enough food to last us for our time there. Despite this we had a great time

– the wind blowing in our faces when we were speeding down the hills, meeting new people, talking in an unfamiliar language and enjoying the beauty of the French countryside.

After completing the challenge Brandon and I took the opportunity to go Paris to learn a bit about French history and look at some of the architecture there which I've been curious to see. We toured the city and visited most of the major attractions. Paris differs to London a lot and is a lively and mystical city especially at night.

Right now I'm back at college finishing my A-levels, having done the challenge I'm passionate to reach the academic goals I have set myself this year. I also plan later on in life to visit France again and to learn French. I would recommend anyone who wants to challenge themselves and has a dream to contact the foundation.

Without the Mark Evison Foundation I could have never done this challenge.

More schools are now participating in the Schools Awards scheme each year, and we hear more inspired accounts of difficult and very diverse challenges, change, growth.

In 2011 we also gave our first Major Award, a more substantial amount of funding: this went to Lee for new equipment to help towards joining the England Canoe Slalom squad. In 2012 we gave Major Awards to a young girl to climb Mt Everest, and to a team of six girls to swim the English Channel.

The Foundation is still very young, and its path is being charted carefully. It now has an endowment fund and its future seems bright. At a time of youth riots, street gangs and disaffected youth, it represents a value system which many applaud and are excited by, particularly the young people themselves and those working with them. Through the Foundation we watch young people become more confident, more experienced, more caring. It does bring out the best in them. It is not being with Mark, but it is being with who he was, his dreams, what mattered to him. I meet Mark again in other young people.

www.markevisonfoundation.org

ROLL OF HONOUR

As at 24 September 2012, a total of 433 British forces personnel or MOD civilians have died whilst serving in Afghanistan since the start of operations in October 2001. Many more have been wounded.

Of these deaths, 390 were killed as a result of hostile action. Forty-three are known to have died either as a result of illness, non-combat injuries or accidents, or have not yet officially been assigned a cause of death pending the outcome of an investigation. The balance of these figures may change as inquests are concluded.

Captain Carl Manley, 41, Royal Marines
Captain James Anthony Townley, 29, from Tunbridge Wells, Corps of Royal Engineers
Sergeant Jonathan Eric Kups, 38, from Nuneaton, Warwickshire, Royal Electrical and Mechanical Engineers
Sergeant Gareth Thursby, 29, from Skipton, 3rd Battalion The Yorkshire Regiment
Private Thomas Wroe, 18, from Huddersfield, 3rd Battalion The Yorkshire Regiment
Lance Corporal Duane Groom, 32, from Suva City, Fiji, 1st Battalion Grenadier Guards
Sergeant Lee Paul Davidson, 32, from Doncaster, The Light Dragoons

Guardsman Karl Whittle, 22, from Bristol, 1st Battalion Grenadier
Guards

Guardsman Jamie Shadrake, 20, from Wrexham, Wales, 1st
Battalion Grenadier Guards

Lance Corporal Matthew David Smith, 26, from Aldershot, Corps
of Royal Engineers

Lieutenant Andrew Robert Chesterman, 26, from Guildford, 3rd
Battalion The Rifles

Warrant Officer Class 2 Leonard Perran Thomas, 44, from Ross-
on-Wye, Royal Corps of Signals

Guardsman Craig Andrew Roderick, 22, from Cardiff, 1st
Battalion Welsh Guards

Guardsman Apete Saunikalou Ratumaiyale Tuisovurua, 28, from
Fiji, 1st Battalion Welsh Guards

Corporal Alex Guy, 37, from St Neots, Cambridgeshire, 1st
Battalion The Royal Anglian Regiment

Lance Corporal James Ashworth, 23, from Kettering, 1st Battalion
Grenadier Guards

Private Gregg Thomas Stone, 20, from Yorkshire, 3rd Battalion The
Yorkshire Regiment

Corporal Michael John Thacker, 27, from Swindon, Wiltshire, 1st
Battalion The Royal Welsh

Captain Stephen James Healey, 29, from Cardiff, 1st Battalion The
Royal Welsh

Corporal Brent John McCarthy, 25, from Priorslee, Telford, Royal
Air Force

Lance Corporal Lee Thomas Davies, 27, from Carmarthen, 1st
Battalion Welsh Guards

Corporal Andrew Steven Roberts, 32, from Middlesbrough, 23
Pioneer Regiment The Royal Logistic Corps

Private Ratu Manasa Silibaravi, 32, from Fiji, 23 Pioneer Regiment
The Royal Logistic Corps

Guardsman Michael Roland, 22, from Worthing, 1st Battalion
Grenadier Guards

Sapper Connor Ray, 21, from Newport, 33 Engineer Regiment
(Explosive Ordnance Disposal)

Corporal Jack Leslie Stanley, 26, from Bolton, The Queen's Royal
Hussars

Sergeant Luke Taylor, 33, from Bournemouth, Royal Marines

Lance Corporal Michael Foley, 25, from Burnley, Lancashire,
Adjutant General's Corps (Staff and Personnel Support)

Captain Rupert William Michael Bowers, 24, from
  Wolverhampton, 2nd Battalion The Mercian Regiment
Sergeant Nigel Coupe, 33, from Lytham Saint Anne's, Lancashire,
  1st Battalion The Duke of Lancaster's Regiment
Corporal Jake Hartley, 20, from Dewsbury, West Yorkshire, 3rd
  Battalion The Yorkshire Regiment
Private Anthony Frampton, 20, from Huddersfield, 3rd Battalion
  The Yorkshire Regiment
Private Christopher Kershaw, 19, from Bradford, 3rd Battalion The
  Yorkshire Regiment
Private Daniel Wade, 20, from Warrington, 3rd Battalion The
  Yorkshire Regiment
Private Daniel Wilford, 21, from Huddersfield, 3rd Battalion The
  Yorkshire Regiment
Senior Aircraftman Ryan Tomlin, 21, from Hemel Hempstead, 2
  Squadron RAF Regiment
Lance Corporal Gajbahadur Gurung, 26, from Majthana, Nepal,
  Royal Gurkha Rifles
Signaller Ian Gerard Sartorius-Jones, 21, from Runcorn, Cheshire,
  20th Armoured Brigade Headquarters and Signal Squadron
  (200)
Rifleman Sachin Limbu, 23, from Rajghat, Morang in Nepal, 1st
  Battalion The Royal Gurkha Rifles
Private John King, 19, from Darlington, 1st Battalion The Yorkshire
  Regiment
Squadron Leader Anthony Downing, 34, from Kent, Royal Air
  Force
Captain Tom Jennings, 29, Royal Marines
Sapper Elijah Bond, 24, from St Austell, 35 Engineer Regiment
  Royal Engineers
Rifleman Sheldon Lee Jordan Steel, 20, from Leeds, 5th Battalion
  The Rifles
Private Thomas Christopher Lake, 29, from Watford, 1st Battalion
  The Princess of Wales's Royal Regiment
Lieutenant David Boyce, 25, from Welwyn Garden City, Herts, 1st
  The Queen's Dragoon Guards
Lance Corporal Richard Scanlon, 31, from Rhymney, Gwent, 1st
  The Queen's Dragoon Guards
Lance Corporal Peter Eustace, 25, from Liverpool, 2nd Battalion
  The Rifles

Private Matthew Thornton, 28, from Barnsley, 4th Battalion The Yorkshire Regiment

Private Matthew James Sean Haseldin, 21, from Settle, Yorkshire, 2nd Battalion The Mercian Regiment

Rifleman Vijay Rai, 21, from the Bhojpur District, Deaurali in the East of Nepal, 2nd Battalion The Royal Gurkha Rifles

Marine David Fairbrother, 24, from Blackburn, Kilo Company 42 Commando Royal Marines

Lance Corporal Jonathan James McKinlay, 33, from Darlington, County Durham, 1st Battalion The Rifles

Sergeant Barry John Weston, 40, from Reading, Kilo Company 42 Commando Royal Marines

Lieutenant Daniel John Clack, 24, from London, 1st Battalion The Rifles

Marine James Robert Wright, 22, from Weymouth, 42 Commando Royal Marines

Corporal Mark Anthony Palin, 32, from Plymouth, 1st Battalion The Rifles

Lance Corporal Paul Watkins, 24, from Port Elizabeth, Republic of South Africa, from 9th/12th Royal Lancers (Prince of Wales's)

Highlander Scott McLaren, 20, from Edinburgh, The Highlanders 4th Battalion The Royal Regiment of Scotland

Private Gareth Leslie William Bellingham, 22, from Stoke-on-Trent, 3rd Battalion The Mercian Regiment (Staffords)

Corporal Lloyd Newell, The Parachute Regiment

Craftsman Andrew Found, 27, from Whitby, Royal Electrical and Mechanical Engineers

Rifleman Martin Jon Lamb, 27, from Gloucester, 1st Battalion The Rifles

Lance Corporal Martin Joseph Gill, 22, from Nottingham, 42 Commando Royal Marines

Corporal Michael John Pike, 26, from Huntly, Scotland, The Highlanders 4th Battalion The Royal Regiment of Scotland

Lieutenant Oliver Richard Augustin, 23, from Kent, Juliet Company 42 Commando Royal Marines

Marine Samuel Giles William Alexander MC, 28, from London, Juliet Company 42 Commando Royal Marines

Colour Serjeant Kevin Charles Fortuna, 36, from Cheltenham, A Company 1st Battalion The Rifles

Marine Nigel Dean Mead, 19, from Carmarthen, 42 Commando Royal Marines

Captain Lisa Jade Head, 29, from Huddersfield, 11 EOD Regiment
RLC

Colour Sergeant Alan Cameron, 42, from Livingston, Scotland, 1st
Battalion Scots Guards

Major Matthew James Collins, 38, from Backwell, Somerset, 1st
Battalion Irish Guards

Lance Sergeant Mark Terence Burgan, 28, from Liverpool, 1st
Battalion Irish Guards

Private Daniel Steven Prior, 27, from Peacehaven, East Sussex, 2nd
Battalion The Parachute Regiment

Lance Corporal McKee, 27, from Banbridge, County Down,
Northern Ireland, 1st Battalion The Royal Irish Regiment

Lance Corporal Liam Richard Tasker, 26, from Kirkcaldy, Fife,
Scotland, Royal Army Veterinary Corps

Private Robert Wood, 28, from Hampshire, 17 Port and Maritime
Regiment Royal Logistic Corps

Private Dean Hutchinson, 23, from Wiltshire, 9 Regiment The
Royal Logistic Corps

Lance Corporal Kyle Cleet Marshall, 23, from Newcastle, 2nd
Battalion The Parachute Regiment

Private Lewis Hendry, 20, from Norwich, 3rd Battalion The
Parachute Regiment

Private Conrad Lewis, 22, from Bournemouth, 4th Battalion The
Parachute Regiment

Warrant Officer Class 2 (Company Sergeant Major) Colin
Beckett, 36, from Peterborough, 3rd Battalion The Parachute
Regiment

Ranger David Dalzell, 20, from Bangor, County Down, Northern
Ireland, 1st Battalion The Royal Irish Regiment

Private Martin Simon George Bell, 24, from Bradford, 2nd
Battalion The Parachute Regiment

Private Joseva Saqanagonedau Vatubua, 24, from Suva, Fiji, 5th
Battalion The Royal Regiment of Scotland

Warrant Officer Class 2 Charles Henry Wood, 34, from
Middlesborough, 23 Pioneer Regiment Royal Logistic Corps,
serving with the Counter-Improvised Explosive Device
Task Force

Corporal Steven Thomas Dunn, 27, from Gateshead, 216
(Parachute) Signal Squadron, attached to 2nd Battalion the
Parachute Regiment Battlegroup

Private John Howard, 23, from Wellington, New Zealand, 3rd
  Battalion The Parachute Regiment
Guardsman Christopher Davies, 22, from St Helens, Merseyside,
  1st Battalion Irish Guards
Ranger Aaron McCormick, 22, from Coleraine, County
  Londonderry, Northern Ireland, 1st Battalion The Royal Irish
  Regiment
Senior Aircraftman Scott 'Scotty' Hughes, 20, from North Wales, 1
  Squadron Royal Air Force Regiment
Sapper William Bernard Blanchard, 39, from Gosport, Hampshire,
  101 (City of London) Engineer Regiment (Explosive Ordnance
  Disposal)
Corporal David Barnsdale, 24, from Tring, 33 Engineer Regiment
Sergeant Peter Anthony Rayner, 34, from Bradford, 2nd Battalion
  The Duke of Lancaster's Regiment
Rifleman Suraj Gurung, 22, from Gorkha, Nepal, 1st Battalion The
  Royal Gurkha Rifles
Corporal Matthew Thomas, 24, from Swansea, Royal Electrical
  and Mechanical Engineers
Sergeant Andrew James Jones, 35, from Newport, South Wales,
  Royal Engineers
Trooper Andrew Martin Howarth, 20, from Bournemouth, The
  Queen's Royal Lancers
Kingsman Darren Deady, 22, from Bolton, 2nd Battalion The
  Duke of Lancaster's Regiment
Captain Andrew Griffiths, 25, from Richmond, North Yorkshire,
  2nd Battalion The Duke of Lancaster's Regiment
Lance Corporal Joseph McFarlane Pool, 26, from Greenock, The
  Royal Scots Borderers 1st Battalion The Royal Regiment of
  Scotland
Lance Corporal Jordan Dean Bancroft, 25, from Burnley, 1st
  Battalion The Duke of Lancaster's Regiment
Sapper Ishwor Gurung, 21, from Pokhara, Nepal, 69 Gurkha Field
  Squadron 21 Engineer Regiment
Sapper Darren Foster, 20, from Carlisle, 21 Engineer Regiment
Rifleman Remand Kulung, 27, from Nepal, 1st Battalion The
  Mercian Regiment (Cheshire)
Lieutenant John Charles Sanderson, 29, from Oklahoma, USA, 1st
  Battalion The Mercian Regiment (Cheshire)
Marine Adam Brown, 26, from Burtle, near Glastonbury, 40
  Commando Royal Marines

Lance Sergeant Dale Alanzo McCallum, 31, from Hanover, Jamaica, 1st Battalion Scots Guards

Sapper Mark Antony Smith, 26, from Swanley, Kent, 36 Engineer Regiment

Corporal Matthew James Stenton, 23, from Wakefield, The Royal Dragoon Guards

Lance Corporal Stephen Daniel Monkhouse, 28, from Greenock, 1st Battalion Scots Guards

Staff Sergeant Brett George Linley, 29, from Birmingham, The Royal Logistic Corps

Sergeant David Thomas Monkhouse, 35, from Aspatria, Cumbria, The Royal Dragoon Guards

Senior Aircraftman Kinikki 'Griff' Griffiths, 20, Royal Air Force

Marine Jonathan David Thomas Crookes, 26, from Birmingham, 40 Commando Royal Marines

Marine Matthew Harrison, 23, from Hemel Hempstead, 40 Commando Royal Marines

Major James Joshua Bowman, 34, from Salisbury, 1st Battalion The Royal Gurkha Rifles

Lieutenant Neal Turkington, 26, from Craigavon, 1st Battalion The Royal Gurkha Rifles

Corporal Arjun Purja Pun, 33, from Khibang, Magdi District, Nepal, 1st Battalion The Royal Gurkha Rifles

Marine David Charles Hart, 23, from Upper Poppleton, North Yorkshire, 40 Commando Royal Marines

Bombardier Samuel Joseph Robinson, 31, from Carmarthen, 5th Regiment Royal Artillery

Private Thomas Sephton, 20, from Warrington, 1st Battalion The Mercian Regiment

Trooper James Anthony Leverett, 20, from Sheffield, Royal Dragoon Guards

Corporal Seth Stephens, 42, from Dorset, Special Boat Service, Royal Marines

Corporal Jamie Kirkpatrick, 32, from Llanelli, 101 Engineer Regiment (Explosive Ordnance Disposal)

Bombardier Stephen Raymond Gilbert, 36, from Topcliffe, North Yorkshire, 4th Regiment Royal Artillery

Colour Sergeant Martyn Horton, 34, from Runcorn, 1st Battalion The Mercian Regiment

Lance Corporal David Ramsden, 26, from Leeds, 1st Battalion The Yorkshire Regiment

Private Douglas Halliday, 20, from Wallasey, Merseyside, 1st
Battalion The Mercian Regiment

Private Alex Isaac, 20, from the Wirral, 1st Battalion The Mercian
Regiment

Sergeant Steven William Darbyshire, 35, from Wigan, 40
Commando Royal Marines

Lance Corporal Michael Taylor, 30, from Rhyl, Charlie Company
40 Commando Royal Marines

Marine Paul Warren, 23, from Leyland, Lancashire, 40 Commando
Royal Marines

Marine Richard Hollington, 23, from Petersfield, 40 Commando
Royal Marines

Trooper Ashley Smith, 21, from York, Royal Dragoon Guards

Corporal Taniela Tolevu Rogoiruwai, 32, from Nausori, Fiji, 1st
Battalion The Duke of Lancaster's Regiment, serving as part of
Combined Force Nad 'Ali

Kingsman Ponipate Tagitaginimoce, 29, from Nausori, Fiji, 1st
Battalion The Duke of Lancaster's Regiment, serving as part of
Combined Force Nad 'Ali

Marine Steven James Birdsall, 20, from Warrington, 40
Commando Royal Marines

Lance Corporal Andrew Breeze, 31, from Manchester, B (Malta)
Company 1st Battalion The Mercian Regiment (Cheshire)

Private Jonathan Michael Monk, 25, from London, 2nd Battalion
The Princess of Wales's Royal Regiment

Lance Bombardier Mark Chandler, 32, from Nailsworth,
Gloucestershire, 3rd Regiment Royal Horse Artillery

Corporal Terry Webster, 24, from Chester, 1st Battalion The
Mercian Regiment (Cheshire)

Lance Corporal Alan Cochran, 23, from St Asaph, North Wales,
1st Battalion The Mercian Regiment (Cheshire)

Marine Anthony Dean Hotine, 21, from Warminster, 40
Commando Royal Marines

Marine Scott Gregory Taylor, 20, from Buxton, 40 Commando
Royal Marines

Corporal Stephen Paul Curley, 26, from Exeter, 40 Commando
Royal Marines

Gunner Zak Cusack, 20, from Stoke-on-Trent, 4th Regiment
Royal Artillery

Corporal Stephen Walker, 42, from Lisburn, Northern Ireland, 40
Commando Royal Marines

Corporal Christopher Lewis Harrison, 26, from Watford, 40 Commando Royal Marines

Sapper Daryn Roy, 28, from Consett, County Durham, 21 Engineer Regiment

Lance Corporal Barry Buxton, 27, from Meir, Stoke-on-Trent, 21 Engineer Regiment

Corporal Harvey Holmes, 22, from Hyde, Greater Manchester, 1st Battalion The Mercian Regiment

Fusilier Jonathan Burgess, 20, from Townhill, Swansea, 1st Battalion The Royal Welsh

Rifleman Mark Turner, 21, from Gateshead, 3rd Battalion The Rifles

Guardsman Michael Sweeney, 19, from Blyth, Northumberland, 1st Battalion Coldstream Guards

Rifleman Daniel Holkham, 19, from Chatham, Kent, 3rd Battalion The Rifles

Lance Corporal of Horse Jonathan Woodgate, 26, from Lavenham, Suffolk, Household Cavalry Regiment

Serjeant Steven Campbell, 30, from Durham, 3rd Battalion The Rifles

Lance Corporal Scott Hardy, 26, from Chelmsford, 1st Battalion The Royal Anglian Regiment

Private James Grigg, 20, from Hartismere, Suffolk, 1st Battalion The Royal Anglian Regiment

Captain Martin Driver, 31, from Barnsley, 1st Battalion The Royal Anglian Regiment

Corporal Stephen Thompson, 31, from Bovey Tracey, Devon, 1st Battalion The Rifles

Lance Corporal Tom Keogh, 24, from Paddington, London, 4th Battalion The Rifles

Rifleman Liam Maughan, 18, from Doncaster, 3rd Battalion The Rifles

Rifleman Jonathon Allott, 19, from North Shields, 3rd Battalion the Rifles

Corporal Richard Green, 23, from Reading, 3rd Battalion The Rifles

Rifleman Carlo Apolis, 28, from South Africa, 4th Battalion The Rifles

Sergeant Paul Fox, 34, from St Ives, 28 Engineer Regiment

Rifleman Martin Kinggett, 19, from Dagenham, 4th Battalion The Rifles

Senior Aircraftman Luke Southgate, 20, from Bury St Edmunds,
II Squadron Royal Air Force Regiment

Lance Sergeant David 'Davey' Walker, 36, from Glasgow, 1st
Battalion Scots Guards

Lieutenant Douglas Dalzell, 27, Berkshire, 1st Battalion
Coldstream Guards

Sapper Guy Mellors, 20, from Coventry, 36 Engineer Regiment

Kingsman Sean Dawson, 19, from Ashton-Under-Lyne,
Manchester, 2nd Battalion The Duke of Lancaster's Regiment

Rifleman Mark Marshall, 29, from Exeter, 6th Battalion The Rifles

Lance Sergeant Dave Greenhalgh, 25, from Ilkeston, Derbyshire,
1st Battalion Grenadier Guards

Lance Corporal Darren Hicks, 29, from Mousehole, Cornwall, 1st
Battalion Coldstream Guards

Warrant Officer Class 2 David Markland, 36, from Euxton,
Lancashire, 36 Engineer Regiment

Corporal John Moore, 22, from Lanarkshire, The Royal Scots
Borderers 1st Battalion The Royal Regiment of Scotland

Private Sean McDonald, 26, from Edinburgh, The Royal Scots
Borderers 1st Battalion The Royal Regiment of Scotland

Corporal Liam Riley, 21, from Sheffield, 3rd Battalion The
Yorkshire Regiment

Lance Corporal Graham Shaw, 27, from Huddersfield, 3rd
Battalion The Yorkshire Regiment

Lance Corporal Daniel Cooper, 22, from Hereford, 3rd Battalion
The Rifles

Rifleman Peter Aldridge, 19, from Folkestone, Kent, 4th Battalion
The Rifles

Corporal Lee Brownson, 30, from Bishop Auckland, 3rd Battalion
The Rifles

Rifleman Luke Farmer, 19, from Pontefract, 3rd Battalion The
Rifles

Captain Daniel Read, 31, from Rainham, Kent, 11 Explosive
Ordnance Disposal Regiment Royal Logistic Corps

Private Robert Hayes, 19, from Cambridge, 1st Battalion The Royal
Anglian Regiment

Sapper David Watson, 23, from Tyne and Wear, 33 Engineer
Regiment (Explosive Ordnance Disposal)

Rifleman Aidan Howell, 19, from Sidcup, Kent, 3rd Battalion The
Rifles

Lance Corporal Tommy Brown, 25, from Glasgow, The Parachute
Regiment

Lance Corporal Christopher Roney, 23, from Sunderland, A
Company 3rd Battalion The Rifles

Lance Corporal Michael David Pritchard, 22, from Maidstone, 4th
Regiment Royal Military Police

Corporal Simon Hornby, 29, from Liverpool, 2nd Battalion The
Duke of Lancaster's Regiment

Lance Corporal David Leslie Kirkness, 24, from West Yorkshire,
3rd Battalion The Rifles

Rifleman James Stephen Brown, 18, from Kent, 3rd Battalion The
Rifles

Lance Corporal Adam Drane, 23, from Bury St Edmunds, 1st
Battalion The Royal Anglian Regiment

Acting Sergeant John Paxton Amer, 30, from Sunderland, 1st
Battalion Coldstream Guards

Sergeant Robert David Loughran-Dickson, 33, from Deal, Kent,
4th Regiment Royal Military Police

Corporal Loren Owen Christopher Marlton-Thomas, 28, from
Braintree, Essex, 33 Engineer Regiment (EOD)

Rifleman Andrew Ian Fentiman, 23, from Cambridge, 7th
Battalion The Rifles

Rifleman Samuel John Bassett, 20, from Plymouth, 4th Battalion
The Rifles

Rifleman Philip Allen, 20, from Dorset, 2nd Battalion The Rifles

Serjeant Phillip Scott, 30, from Malton, 3rd Battalion The Rifles

Warrant Officer Class 1 Darren Chant, 40, from Walthamstow, 1st
Battalion The Grenadier Guards

Sergeant Matthew Telford, 37, from Grimsby, 1st Battalion The
Grenadier Guards

Guardsman James Major, 18, from Grimsby, 1st Battalion The
Grenadier Guards

Corporal Steven Boote, 22, from Birkenhead, Liverpool, Royal
Military Police

Corporal Nicholas Webster-Smith, 24, from Glangwili, Royal
Military Police

Staff Sergeant Olaf Sean George Schmid, 30, from Truro, Royal
Logistic Corps

Corporal Thomas 'Tam' Mason, 27, from Rosyth, The Black Watch
3rd Battalion The Royal Regiment of Scotland

Corporal James Oakland, 26, from Manchester, Royal Military
Police

Lance Corporal James Hill, 23, from Redhill, Surrey, 1st Battalion
Coldstream Guards

Guardsman Jamie Janes, 20, from Brighton, 1st Battalion
Grenadier Guards

Acting Corporal Marcin Wojtak, 24, from Leicester, 34 Squadron
RAF Regiment

Private James Prosser, 21, from Cwmbran, 2nd Battalion The Royal
Welsh

Acting Sergeant Michael Lockett MC, 29, from Monifieth, Angus,
2nd Battalion The Mercian Regiment

Acting Sergeant Stuart McGrath, 28, from Buckinghamshire, 2nd
Battalion The Rifles

Trooper Brett Hall, 21, from Dartmouth, 2nd Royal Tank
Regiment

Kingsman Jason Dunn-Bridgeman, 20, from Liverpool, 2nd
Battalion The Duke of Lancaster's Regiment

Corporal John Harrison, 29, from East Kilbride, Lanarkshire, The
Parachute Regiment

Private Gavin Elliott, 19, from Woodsetts, Worksop,
Nottinghamshire, 2nd Battalion The Mercian Regiment

Lance Corporal Richard Brandon, 24, from Kidderminster, Royal
Electrical and Mechanical Engineers

Sergeant Stuart 'Gus' Millar, 40, from Inverness, The Black Watch
3rd Battalion The Royal Regiment of Scotland

Private Kevin Elliott, 24, from Dundee, The Black Watch 3rd
Battalion The Royal Regiment of Scotland

Sergeant Lee Andrew Houltram, 33, Royal Marines

Fusilier Shaun Bush, 24, from Warwickshire, 2nd Battalion The
Royal Regiment of Fusiliers

Serjeant Paul McAleese, 29, from Hereford, 2nd Battalion The
Rifles

Private Johnathon Young, 18, from Hull, 3rd Battalion The
Yorkshire Regiment (Duke of Wellington's)

Lance Corporal James Fullarton, 24, from Coventry, 2nd Battalion
The Royal Regiment of Fusiliers

Fusilier Simon Annis, 22, from Salford, Greater Manchester, 2nd
Battalion The Royal Regiment of Fusiliers

Fusilier Louis Carter, 18, from Nuneaton, 2nd Battalion The Royal
Regiment of Fusiliers

Sergeant Simon Valentine, 29, from Bedworth, 2nd Battalion The
Royal Regiment of Fusiliers

Private Richard Hunt, 21, from Abergavenny, 2nd Battalion The
Royal Welsh

Captain Mark Hale, 42, from Bournemouth, 2nd Battalion The
Rifles

Lance Bombardier Matthew Hatton, 23, from Easingwold, North
Yorkshire, 40th Regiment Royal Artillery (The Lowland
Gunners)

Rifleman Daniel Wild, 19, from Hartlepool, 2nd Battalion The
Rifles

Private Jason George Williams, 23, from Worcester, 2nd Battalion
The Mercian Regiment

Corporal Kevin Mulligan, 26, The Parachute Regiment

Lance Corporal Dale Thomas Hopkins, 23, The Parachute
Regiment

Private Kyle Adams, 21, The Parachute Regiment

Craftsman Anthony Lombardi, 21, from Scunthorpe, Royal
Electrical and Mechanical Engineers (REME), attached to The
Light Dragoons

Trooper Phillip Lawrence, 22, from Birkenhead, Light Dragoons

Warrant Officer Class 2 Sean Upton, 35, from Nottinghamshire,
5th Regiment Royal Artillery

Bombardier Craig Hopson, 24, from Castleford, 40th Regiment
Royal Artillery (The Lowland Gunners)

Guardsman Christopher King, 20, from Birkenhead, near
Liverpool, 1st Battalion Coldstream Guards

Captain Daniel Shepherd, 28, from Lincoln, 11 Explosive
Ordnance Disposal Regiment The Royal Logistic Corps

Corporal Joseph Etchells, 22, from Mossley, 2nd Battalion The
Royal Regiment of Fusiliers

Rifleman Aminiasi Toge, 26, from Suva, Fiji, 2nd Battalion The
Rifles

Corporal Jonathan Horne, 28, from Walsall, 2nd Battalion The
Rifles

Rifleman William Aldridge, 18, from Bromyard, Herefordshire,
2nd Battalion The Rifles

Rifleman James Backhouse, 18, from Castleford, Yorkshire, 2nd
Battalion The Rifles

Rifleman Joe Murphy, 18, from Castle Bromwich, Birmingham,
2nd Battalion The Rifles

Rifleman Daniel Simpson, 20, from Croydon, 2nd Battalion The Rifles

Corporal Lee Scott, 26, from Kings Lynn, 2nd Royal Tank Regiment

Private John Brackpool, 27, from Crawley, West Sussex, 1st Battalion Welsh Guards

Rifleman Daniel Hume, 22, from Berkshire, 4th Battalion The Rifles

Trooper Christopher Whiteside, 20, from Blackpool, The Light Dragoons

Captain Ben Babington-Browne, 27, from Maidstone, 22 Engineer Regiment Royal Engineers

Lance Corporal Dane Elson, 22, from Bridgend, 1st Battalion Welsh Guards

Lance Corporal David Dennis, 29, from Llanelli, Wales, The Light Dragoons

Private Robert Laws, 18, from Bromsgrove, Worcestershire, 2nd Battalion the Mercian Regiment

Lieutenant Colonel Rupert Thorneloe MBE, 39, from Kirtlington, Commanding Officer, 1st Battalion Welsh Guards

Trooper Joshua Hammond, 18, from Plymouth, 2nd Royal Tank Regiment

Major Sean Birchall, 33, from Guildford, 30, from Cromer, 1st Battalion Welsh Guards

Lieutenant Paul Mervis, 27, from London, 2nd Battalion The Rifles

Private Robert McLaren, 20, from the Isle of Mull, The Black Watch 3rd Battalion The Royal Regiment of Scotland

Rifleman Cyrus Thatcher, 19, from Reading, 2nd Battalion The Rifles

Lance Corporal Nigel Moffett, 28, from Belfast, The Light Dragoons

Corporal Stephen Bolger, 30, from Cromer, Norfolk, The Parachute Regiment

Lance Corporal Kieron Hill, 20, from Nottingham, 2nd Battalion The Mercian Regiment (Worcesters and Foresters)

Lance Corporal Robert Martin Richards, 24, from Betws-y-Coed, North Wales, Armoured Support Group Royal Marines

Sapper Jordan Rossi, 22, from Conwy, West Yorkshire, 25 Field Squadron 38 Engineer Regiment

Fusilier Petero 'Pat' Suesue, 28, from Fiji, 2nd Battalion The Royal Regiment of Fusiliers

Marine Jason Mackie, 21, from Bampton, Oxfordshire, Armoured Support Group Royal Marines

Lieutenant Mark Evison, 26, from London, 1st Battalion Welsh Guards

Sergeant Ben Ross, 34, from Bangor, 173 Provost Company 3rd Regiment Royal Military Police

Corporal Kumar Pun, 31, from Nepal, The 1st Battalion The Royal Gurkha Rifles

Rifleman Adrian Sheldon, 25, from Kirkby-in-Ashfield, 2nd Battalion The Rifles

Corporal Sean Binnie, 22, from Dublin, Republic of Ireland, 3rd Battalion, Royal Regiment of Scotland

Lance Sergeant Tobie Fasfous, 29, from Bridgend, 1st Battalion Welsh Guards

Corporal Dean Thomas John, 25, from Port Talbot, Royal Electrical and Mechanical Engineers

Corporal Graeme Stiff, 24, from Münster, Germany, Royal Electrical and Mechanical Engineers

Lance Corporal Christopher Harkett, 22, from Swansea, 2nd Battalion The Royal Welsh

Marine Michael 'Mick' Laski, 21, from Liverpool, 45 Commando Royal Marines

Corporal Tom Gaden, 24, from Taunton, 1st Battalion The Rifles

Lance Corporal Paul Upton, 31, from Looe, Cornwall, 1st Battalion The Rifles

Rifleman Jamie Gunn, 21, from Leamington Spa, 1st Battalion The Rifles

Lance Corporal Stephen 'Schnoz' Kingscott, 22, from Plymouth, 1st Battalion The Rifles

Marine Darren 'Daz' Smith, 27, from Fleetwood, Lancashire, 45 Commando Royal Marines

Corporal Daniel 'Danny' Nield, 31, from Cheltenham, 1st Battalion The Rifles

Acting Corporal Richard 'Robbo' Robinson, 21, from Cornwall, 1st Battalion The Rifles

Captain Tom Sawyer, 26, from Hertfordshire, 29 Commando Regiment Royal Artillery

Corporal Danny Winter, 28, from Stockport, 45 Commando Royal Marines

Marine Travis Mackin, 22, from Plymouth, Communications Squadron, United Kingdom Landing Force Command Support Group

Serjeant Chris Reed, 25, from Plymouth, 6th Battalion The Rifles

Corporal Liam Elms RM, 26, from Wigan, 45 Commando Royal
Marines

Lance Corporal Benjamin Whatley, 20, from King's Lynn, 42
Commando Royal Marines

Corporal Robert Deering, 33, from Solihull, Commando Logistic
Regiment Royal Marines

Rifleman Stuart Nash, 21, from Sydney, Australia, 1st Battalion The
Rifles

Lieutenant Aaron Lewis, 26, from Essex, 29 Commando Regiment
Royal Artillery

Lance Corporal Steven 'Jamie' Fellows, 28, from Sheffield, 45
Commando Royal Marines

Marine Damian Davies, 27, from Telford, Commando Logistics
Regiment

Sergeant John Manuel, 38, from Tyne and Wear, 45 Commando

Corporal Marc Birch, 26, from Northampton, 45 Commando

Marine Tony Evans, 20, from Sunderland, 42 Commando Royal
Marines

Marine Georgie Sparks, 19, from Epping, 42 Commando Royal
Marines

Marine Alexander Lucas, 24 from Edinburgh, 45 Commando
Royal Marines

Colour Sergeant Krishnabahadur Dura, 36, from Lamjung district,
western Nepal, 2nd Battalion The Royal Gurkha Rifles

Marine Neil David Dunstan, 32, from Bournemouth, 3
Commando Brigade

Marine Robert Joseph McKibben, 32, from County Mayo, Ireland,
3 Commando Brigade

Rifleman Yubraj Rai, 2nd Battalion, 28, from Khotang district,
Nepal, The Royal Gurkha Rifles

Trooper James Munday, D Squadron, 21, from Birmingham, The
Household Cavalry Regiment

Lance Corporal Nicky Mason, 26, from Aveley, Essex, 2nd
Battalion The Parachute Regiment

Private Jason Lee Rawstron, 23, from Lancashire, 2nd Battalion
The Parachute Regiment

Warrant Officer Class 2 Gary 'Gaz' O'Donnell GM, 40, from
Edinburgh, 11 Explosive Ordnance Disposal Regiment Royal
Logistic Corps

Ranger Justin James Cupples, 29, from County Cavan, Ireland, 1st
Battalion The Royal Irish Regiment

Corporal Barry Dempsey, 29, from Ayrshire, The Royal Highland
Fusiliers 2nd Battalion Royal Regiment of Scotland

Signaller Wayne Bland, 21, from Leeds, 16 Signal Regiment

Private Peter Joe Cowton, 25, from Basingstoke, 2nd Battalion The
Parachute Regiment

Sergeant Jonathan Mathews, 35, from Edinburgh, The Highlanders
4th Battalion The Royal Regiment of Scotland

Lance Corporal Kenneth Michael Rowe, 24, from Newcastle,
Royal Army Veterinary Corps

Corporal Jason Stuart Barnes, 25, from Exeter, Royal Electrical and
Mechanical Engineers

Lance Corporal James Johnson, 31, from Scotland, B Company 5th
Battalion The Royal Regiment of Scotland

Warrant Officer 2nd Class Dan Shirley, 32, from Leicester, Air
Assault Support Regiment Royal Logistics Corps

Warrant Officer 2nd Class Michael Norman Williams, 40, from
Cardiff, 2nd Battalion The Parachute Regiment

Private Joe John Whittaker, 20, from Stratford Upon Avon, 4th
Battalion The Parachute Regiment

Corporal Sarah Bryant, 26, from Carlisle, Intelligence Corps

Corporal Sean Robert Reeve, 28, from Brighton, Royal Signals

Lance Corporal Richard Larkin, 39, from Cookley, Special Air
Service

Paul Stout, 31, Special Air Service

Lance Corporal James Bateman, 29, from Staines, Middlesex, 2nd
Battalion The Parachute Regiment

Private Jeff Doherty, 20, from Southam, Warwickshire, 2nd
Battalion The Parachute Regiment

Private Nathan Cuthbertson, 19, from Sunderland, 2nd Battalion
The Parachute Regiment

Private Daniel Gamble, 22, from Uckfield, East Sussex, 2nd
Battalion The Parachute Regiment

Private Charles David Murray, 19, from Carlisle, 2nd Battalion The
Parachute Regiment

Marine Dale Gostick, 22, from Oxford, 3 Troop Armoured
Support Company Royal Marines

James Thompson, 27, from Whitley Bay, Army

Trooper Ratu Sakeasi Babakobau, 29, from Fiji, Household
Cavalry Regiment

Trooper Robert Pearson, 22, from Grimsby, The Queen's Royal
Lancers Regiment

Senior Aircraftman Graham Livingstone, 23, from Glasgow, Royal Air Force Regiment

Senior Aircraftman Gary Thompson, 51, from Nottingham, Royal Auxiliary Air Force Regiment

Lieutenant John Thornton, 22, from Ferndown, 40 Commando Royal Marines

Marine David Marsh, 23, from Sheffield, 40 Commando Royal Marines

Corporal Damian Mulvihill, 32, from Plymouth, 40 Commando Royal Marines

Corporal Damian Stephen Lawrence, 25, from Whitby, 2nd Battalion The Yorkshire Regiment (Green Howards)

Corporal Darryl Gardiner, 25, from Salisbury, Wiltshire, Royal Electrical and Mechanical Engineers

Sergeant Lee Johnson, 33, from Stockton-on-Tees, 2nd Battalion The Yorkshire Regiment

Trooper Jack Sadler, 21, from Exeter, The Honourable Artillery Company

Captain John McDermid, 43, from Glasgow, The Royal Highland Fusiliers 2nd Battalion The Royal Regiment of Scotland

Lance Corporal Jake Alderton, 22, from Bexley, 36 Engineer Regiment

Major Alexis Roberts, 32, from Kent, 1st Battalion The Royal Gurkha Rifles

Colour Sergeant Phillip Newman, 36, from Coventry, 4th Battalion The Mercian Regiment

Private Brian Tunnicliffe, 33, from Ilkeston, 2nd Battalion The Mercian Regiment (Worcesters and Foresters)

Corporal Ivano Violino, 29, from Salford, 36 Engineer Regiment

Sergeant Craig Brelsford, 25, from Nottingham, 2nd Battalion The Mercian Regiment

Private Johan Botha, 25, from South Africa, 2nd Battalion The Mercian Regiment

Private Damian Wright, 23, from Mansfield, 2nd Battalion The Mercian Regiment

Private Ben Ford, 18, from Chesterfield, 2nd Battalion The Mercian Regiment

Senior Aircraftman Christopher Bridge, 20, from Sheffield, C flight 51 Squadron Royal Air Force Regiment

Private Aaron James McClure, 19, from Ipswich, 1st Battalion The Royal Anglian Regiment

Private Robert Graham Foster, 19, from Harlow, 1st Battalion The Royal Anglian Regiment

Private John Thrumble, 21, from Chelmsford, 1st Battalion The Royal Anglian Regiment

Captain David Hicks, 26, from Surrey, 1st Battalion The Royal Anglian Regiment

Private Tony Rawson, 27, from Dagenham, Essex, 1st Battalion The Royal Anglian Regiment

Lance Corporal Michael Jones, 26, from Newbald, Yorkshire, Royal Marines

Sergeant Barry Keen, 34, from Gateshead, 14 Signal Regiment

Guardsman David Atherton, 25, from Manchester, 1st Battalion Grenadier Guards

Lance Corporal Alex Hawkins, 22, from East Dereham, Norfolk, 1st Battalion The Royal Anglian Regiment

Guardsman Daryl Hickey, 27, from Birmingham, 1st Battalion Grenadier Guards

Sergeant Dave Wilkinson, 33, from Ashford, Kent, 19 Regiment Royal Artillery

Captain Sean Dolan, 40, from the West Midlands, 1st Battalion The Worcestershire and Sherwood Foresters

Drummer Thomas Wright, 21, from Ripley, Derbyshire, 1st Battalion The Worcestershire and Sherwood Foresters

Guardsman Neil 'Tony' Downes, 20, from Manchester, 1st Battalion Grenadier Guards

Lance Corporal Paul 'Sandy' Sandford, 23, from Nottingham, 1st Battalion The Worcestershire and Sherwood Foresters

Corporal Mike Gilyeat, 28, from Stockport, Royal Military Police

Corporal Darren Bonner, 31, from Norfolk, 1st Battalion The Royal Anglian Regiment

Guardsman Daniel Probyn, 22, from Tipton, 1st Battalion Grenadier Guards

Lance Corporal George Russell Davey, 23, from Suffolk, 1st Battalion The Royal Anglian Regiment

Guardsman Simon Davison, 22, from Newcastle-Upon-Tyne, 1st Battalion Grenadier Guards

Private Chris Gray, 19, from Leicestershire, A Company 1st Battalion The Royal Anglian Regiment

Warrant Officer Class 2, Michael 'Mick' Smith, 39, from Liverpool, 29 Commando Regiment Royal Artillery

Marine Benjamin Reddy, 22, from Ascot, Berkshire, 42
Commando Royal Marines

Lance Bombardier Ross Clark, 25, from South Africa, 29
Commando Regiment Royal Artillery

Lance Bombardier Liam McLaughlin, 21, from Lancashire, 29
Commando Regiment Royal Artillery

Marine Scott Summers, 23, from Crawley, East Sussex, 42
Commando Royal Marines

Marine Jonathan Holland, 23, from Chorley, Lancashire, 45
Commando Royal Marines

Lance Corporal Mathew Ford, 30, from Immingham, Lincolnshire,
45 Commando Royal Marines

Marine Thomas Curry, 21, from London, 42 Commando Royal
Marines

Lance Bombardier James Dwyer, 22, from South Africa, 29
Commando Regiment Royal Artillery

Marine Richard J. Watson, 23, from Caterham, Surrey, 42
Commando Royal Marines

Marine Jonathan Wigley, 21, from Melton Mowbray,
Leicestershire, 45 Commando Royal Marines

Marine Gary Wright, 22, from Glasgow, 45 Commando Royal
Marines

Lance Corporal Paul Muirhead, 29, from Bearley, Warwickshire, 1
Royal Irish Regiment

Lance Corporal Luke McCulloch, 21, from Gillingham, 1 Royal
Irish Regiment

Corporal Mark William Wright, 27, from Edinburgh, 3rd Battalion
The Parachute Regiment

Private Craig O'Donnell, 24, from Clydebank, The Argyll and
Sutherland Highlanders 5th Battalion The Royal Regiment of
Scotland

Flight Lieutenant Steven Johnson, 38, from Collingham,
Nottinghamshire, 120 Squadron

Flight Lieutenant Leigh Anthony Mitchelmore, 28, from
Bournemouth, 120 Squadron

Flight Lieutenant Gareth Rodney Nicholas, 40, from Newquay,
Cornwall

Flight Lieutenant Allan James Squires, 39, from Clatterbridge, 120
Squadron

Flight Lieutenant Steven Swarbrick, 28, from Liverpool, 120
Squadron

Flight Sergeant Gary Wayne Andrews, 48, from Tankerton, Kent, 120 Squadron

Flight Sergeant Stephen Beattie, 42, from Dundee, 120 Squadron

Flight Sergeant Gerard Martin Bell, 48, from Ely, Cambridgeshire, 120 Squadron

Flight Sergeant Adrian Davies, 49, from Amersham, Bucks, 120 Squadron

Sergeant Benjamin James Knight, 25, from Bridgwater, 120 Squadron

Sergeant John Joseph Langton, 29, from Liverpool, 120 Squadron

Sergeant Gary Paul Quilliam, 42, from Manchester, 120 Squadron

Corporal Oliver Simon Dicketts, 27, from Wardhurst, The Parachute Regiment

Marine Joseph David Windall, 22, from Hazlemere, Royal Marines

Ranger Anare Draiva, 27, from Fiji, 1 Royal Irish Regiment

Lance Corporal Jonathan Peter Hetherington, 22, from Port Talbot, 14 Signal Regiment (Electronic Warfare)

Corporal Bryan James Budd, 29, from Ripon, 3rd Battalion The Parachute Regiment

Lance Corporal Sean Tansey, 26, from Washington, Tyne and Wear, The Life Guards

Private Leigh Reeves, 25, from Leicester, Royal Logistic Corps

Private Andrew Barrie Cutts, 19, from Mansfield, Air Assault Support Regiment Royal Logistic Corps

Captain Alex Eida, 29, from Surrey, Royal Horse Artillery

Second Lieutenant Ralph Johnson, 24, from Windsor, Household Cavalry Regiment

Lance Corporal Ross Nicholls, 27, from Edinburgh, Blues and Royals

Private Damien Jackson, 19, from South Shields, Tyne and Wear, 3rd Battalion The Parachute Regiment

Corporal Peter Thorpe, 27, from Barrow-in-Furness, Cumbria, Royal Signals

Lance Corporal Jabron Hashmi, 24, from Birmingham, Intelligence Corps

Captain David Patten, 38, from Londonderry, The Parachute Regiment

Sergeant Paul Bartlett, 35, Royal Marines

Captain Jim Philippson, 29, from St Albans, Hertfordshire, 7 Parachute Regiment Royal Horse Artillery

Lance Corporal Peter Edward Craddock, 31, from Newbury, 1st
  Battalion The Royal Gloucestershire, Berkshire and Wiltshire
  Regiment
Corporal Mark Cridge, 25, 7 Signal Regiment
Lance Corporal Steven Sherwood, 23, from Ross-on-Wye,
  Herefordshire, 1st Battalion, The Royal Gloucestershire,
  Berkshire and Wiltshire Light Infantry
Private Jonathan Kitulagoda, 23, from Clifton, Bedfordshire, The
  Rifle Volunteers
Sergeant Robert Busuttil, 30, from Swansea, Royal Logistic Corps
Corporal John Gregory, 30, from Catterick, Royal Logistic Corps
Private Darren John George, 23 from Pirbright, The Royal Anglian
  Regiment

VERDICT IN THE INQUEST INTO THE DEATH OF LIEUTENANT MARK EVISON

I would like to express my sympathy to Mark's parents and apologise to them for the fact that it has taken so long to hold this inquest.

I am required to do three things in my summing up. The first is to address the law, the second to address the facts and the third is to reach a conclusion and give a verdict.

Law

The purpose of this inquest is to determine who the deceased is, how, when and where he came by his death. In accordance with Rule 42 of the Coroners Rules, I cannot determine any question of civil liability. As Lord Bingham said it is the duty of the Coroner to ensure that the relevant facts are fully investigated. The Coroner should ensure that the relevant facts are exposed to public scrutiny but it is up to the Coroner to set the bounds of the inquiry to be made.

I turn to the Human Rights Act 1998 and to the case of Middleton in 2004. This case determined that in appropriate cases the word 'how' should mean not only how did the person in question come by his death but also by what means and in what circumstances he came by his death. I have heard both Advocates' submissions as to whether I should have treated this inquest as a Middleton inquest. Mr Temple QC, Counsel for Mrs Evison, said that I must treat this as a Middleton inquest. Whilst Mr Farrar for the Ministry of Defence said the opposite. I remain in doubt as to which is correct. However, it is impossible for a Coroner to hold an inquest without knowing from the beginning which type of inquest he is holding. I prepared for this inquest and conducted it as if it was a Middleton inquest, I investigated it on that basis and called witnesses on that basis.

Facts

I have called thirty-eight witnesses over the last few days and have heard all of their evidence.

Lieutenant Mark Evison was twenty-six years old when he died. He was commissioned into the Welsh Guards and deployed to Afghanistan as a Platoon Commander. He arrived in theatre on 15 April 2009, moved to Bastion the next day and moved again to a Forward Operating Post on 21 April 2009. He arrived at Patrol Base Haji-Alem with his platoon on 22 April 2009.

On 9 May 2009, Lieutenant Evison undertook a

patrol with members of the platoon. They left the patrol base at approximately 8.00 a.m. His intention was to check out and secure various identified compounds, disrupt the enemy and dominate the Haji-Alem area. He knew he was likely to come under fire. The patrol checked and secured the first three compounds. The patrol then came under heavy sustained and accurate enemy fire whilst Lieutenant Evison and half of his men were in compound 1. Whilst they were pinned down in compound 1, Lieutenant Evison had difficulty getting connections on his radio. To improve the signal and to get 'eyes on', he moved to the entrance of the compound. There was no door on the entrance to the compound and so he was exposed to the enemy. He was seen by his men to do that twice. This was an extremely brave thing to do and he would have known that he was exposed. On the second occasion he was hit twice by enemy bullets. One was stopped by his body armour but one pierced his body just above the body armour. The bullet entered in his right shoulder and exited from the front of his body. He told his men that he had been shot and told Lance Sergeant Peek to take over command of the platoon.

Guardsman James, the Team Medic, initially treated him as best he could. The wound was bleeding heavily. Guardsman James used the first field dressings that he had to try to stem the bleeding. He did not have Hemcon or Quickclot, which in some circumstances are invaluable in stemming and stopping bleeding. We know from the medical evidence presented during the inquest that they would have not have helped in this case because the artery in the shoulder was severed by the bullet and the only way to stop the bleeding from such an injury was by an operation in an operating theatre.

The platoon medic, Corporal Ben Lacy, was unfortunately pinned down in a ditch on the other side of the track from the compound. Within minutes he crossed the open road under enemy fire to enter the compound and assess Lieutenant Evison's injury. He had Hemcon and other equipment and he used these but was powerless to stop the bleeding and his treatment made no significant difference. Morphine was administered and Lance Sergeant Peek made arrangements to move Mark from the compound to the patrol base so that he could be extracted by helicopter. During the extraction to the patrol base the platoon was under constant fire. There was an attack helicopter at the scene but it could not contribute to the engagement because the crew and the platoon could not positively identify the enemy and to have engaged the enemy would have placed civilians at risk.

Lance Sergeant Peek commanded a successful retreat back to the patrol base. It was both moving and humbling to hear how the soldiers fought their way out and brought Mark back to the patrol base. Guardsman Gizzie was shot through the ankle, the bullet lodging in his other leg. Gunner Gadsby carried Mark and ran across open ground whilst under continuous enemy fire and then went back out of the patrol base to help Guardsman Gizzie. For his actions in this engagement, Gunner Gadsby was awarded the Conspicuous Gallantry Cross.

Sadly, Mark suffered huge blood loss and it was impossible to stop the bleeding without surgery. He required cardiopulmonary resuscitation in the patrol base and was then extracted by helicopter to Camp Bastion. He never regained consciousness. On Sunday 10 May 2009, he was airlifted to Selly Oak Hospital in Birmingham where he died. He was certified dead on 23 May 2009.

I now intend to deal with the evidence in some detail:

Medical Evidence

I will need to consider whether there is any evidence of neglect. Neglect is a term of art in a Coroner's Court. Neglect in a Coroner's Court constitutes gross failure to provide medical attention to a dependant person and there must be a causative link to the person's death. It doesn't need to be the main or only cause, it just has to be a contributing cause.

I have had to consider the involvement of Guardsman James, Corporal Lacy, Guardsman Korosaya, Gunner Gadsby, Guardsman Richards, Guardsman Hobbs and the Afghan National Army Soldier who carried Mark's stretcher. I have also had to consider the people who administered treatment at the patrol base, in the helicopter, at Camp Bastion, and during the flight back to the UK and Selly Oak Hospital.

In relation to Guardsman James, he had no Hemcon or anything similar. The platoon in the field may not have had sufficient fluids to give Mark. I also have to consider whether the Black Hawk helicopter was equipped to deal with Mark's injury. No one has expressed concern about the treatment that Mark received at Camp Bastion or at Selly Oak Hospital. Mr Matthews said that the treatment received at Camp Bastion was indeed remarkable and it was a testament to the treatment received that he had survived so long. He described their efforts at Camp Bastion as nothing short of heroic. I believe that this comment is justified.

Mr Matthews also addressed the concern as to whether Mark's life could have been saved had Guardsman James been equipped with Hemcon or if Corporal Lacy had been equipped with more fluids.

In relation to this point I refer to paragraph 51 of Mr Matthews's report. He says, '*Products like Hemcon may form a gel that has some properties resembling clot on contact with blood and Quickclot is a similar agent. These products would not and could not stop the bleeding from a severed subclavian artery nor would placing these products in the exit wound have been any difference either.*'

Further I refer to paragraph 49 of Mr Matthews's report, '*He was shot through the subclavian artery. This caused massive blood loss. The subclavian artery is a very large artery. Any artery that actually has a name, will bleed catastrophically when cut or severed. The injury to the subclavian artery was at the shoulder and there would not be any "internal bleeding", to use a layman's term. The bleeding would have all been external through his wounds into the tissues external to the chest cavity. Only a vascular surgical clamp across the damaged artery could stop the bleeding. No surgical dressings could possibly have made any difference, be it a Quickclot or other similar dressing.'*

I now refer to the comments made by Lieutenant Colonel Brooks of Camp Bastion Hospital in response to Mr Matthews' comments, *'I agree with the comments re Hemcon or Quickclot – it would not have been of value in this wound or injury pattern'* and *'I agree that nothing in addition could have been done on the helicopter to stop the bleeding. I disagree with the opinion that at the point of CPR commencing that Lt Evison's life could not be saved.'*

Colonel Kemp, please can you speak to Guardsman James and Corporal Lacy and ensure that they understand that there is nothing they could have done to save Mark's life. I am not satisfied that they appreciate that.

I now turn to whether the helicopter was adequately equipped to treat Mark. I refer to Mr Matthews's report at paragraph 54, *'From the witness statements it is not clear to me exactly the state of Lieutenant Evison at quarter past nine. This I believe is a matter for the inquest to determine but if his pulse was becoming un-recordable and required ventilator support by bagging or by cardiopulmonary resuscitation at that time, whilst intravenous resuscitation may have been administered in the helicopter, it would have not been possible to stop the bleeding during the helicopter journey and indeed, as it happened he went into full cardiopulmonary arrest during the helicopter flight and I am of the opinion that at the stage he was requiring cardiopulmonary resuscitation, as a consequence to blood loss, that Lieutenant Evison's life could not effectively be saved, despite the temporary success of heroic attempts to do so.'*

Lieutenant Colonel Brooks agrees that nothing could have been done to stop the bleeding other than by way of surgical intervention but he disagrees that at the time that CPR was administered, Mark's life could not have been saved. Lieutenant Colonel Brooks goes on to say that there is a mortality rate of 50 per cent with those presenting with relatively stable vital signs with this injury at a Unit 1 Trauma Unit. In the circumstances in which Mark sustained his wounds, the mortality rate approaches 100 per cent. Where there is difficulty in extracting the casualty and there is a history of the need for cardiopulmonary resuscitation, the chances of surviving even if the injury was to happen on a doorstep of a hospital in the UK are negligible. Should injury occur on the doorstop of a Level 1 Trauma Unit, there would be a small chance of survival.

Lieutenant Colonel Brooks comments on the delay to the helicopter of 32 or 37 minutes, as variously recorded, *'It is unproven and conjecture that if Lieutenant Evison had received surgical intervention 32 minutes earlier that it would have altered the outcome. In my opinion the suggested*

"32-minute delay" had minimal impact on the chance of survival … The injury occurred in a military contact in Afghanistan, within this context the chance of survival of this injury are minimal. However, I believe that it was correct to make all efforts possible as done.'

Summary of medical evidence

Mark sustained a wound which severed his subclavian artery. The only way the bleeding could be stopped was by the application of a clamp in an operating theatre. Before this could happen, he had to be moved to the patrol base under fire to an irrigation ditch and over an exposed bridge. He had to wait for the helicopter to be authorised to travel and return to Bastion where he would have been taken to the operating theatre to be assessed. Only then could the bleeding be stopped. We are not talking here about small veins leaking, we are talking about a large artery and no surgical dressings could have made a difference. The highest chance of survival any of the doctors have given was minimal based on the belief that where there is life there is hope. We know that Mark's injury was originally assessed by the soldiers as a Category C injury when it should have been a Category B injury. I am entirely satisfied that this wrong categorisation did not contribute to Mark's death. Colonel Kemp, I would like you to make it clear to the relevant soldiers that this did not contribute to Mark's death.

Coroners work on the basis of a balance of probabilities. It is clear that Mark received a very serious wound, which in the circumstances in which it was sustained was more likely than not to result in his death despite all the heroic efforts of his men and of the surgeons at Camp Bastion. I take the point of Mr Temple QC that there is always a chance of survival and that any delay must diminish the chances of survival however minimal. I do not think it's right to move from that position to say that the delay caused his death. I do not find neglect in any medical attention. No one ever suggested that I should record such a finding.

Helicopter delay

The delay to the authorisation of the helicopter has variously been referred to as 32 minutes, 37 minutes and 39 minutes. I will refer to it as 39 minutes as this appears to be the time from the 9-liner to the time when the authorisation was given, the time of the 9-liner being 08:46 and the time of the authorisation for the helicopter being 09:25. Mrs Evison is understandably concerned about this delay and neither the Army nor the Inquest has been able to explain it. I am satisfied that the Army did try to help and that if the documents become available, they will tell the parents and the Court. My concern for this inquest is whether it is more likely than not that this contributed to his death. I do not believe so. I rely on paragraph 54 of Mr Matthews's report, *'From the witness statements it is not clear to me exactly the state of Lieutenant Evison at quarter past nine. This I believe is a matter for the inquest to determine but if his pulse was becoming un-recordable and required ventilator support by bagging or by cardiopulmonary resuscitation at that time, whilst intravenous resuscitation may have been adminis- tered in the helicopter, it would have not been possible to stop the bleeding during the helicopter journey and indeed, as it happened he went into full cardiopulmonary arrest during the helicopter flight and I am of the opinion that at the stage he was requiring cardiopulmonary resuscitation, as a conse- quence to blood loss, that Lieutenant Evison's life could not effectively be saved, despite the temporary success of heroic attempts to do so.'*

Mr Matthews also said in paragraph 57 of his report, *'The guidance I can give the inquest is that I am of the opinion that by the time Lieutenant Mark Evison was beginning to drift in and out of consciousness, he was unsal- vageable without advanced resuscitative techniques. By the time he required cardiopulmonary support, on the balance of probabilities, long-term survival was not a realistic expecta- tion and even if that were not so, the hypoxic brain injury in association with this state of affairs, would have rendered him requiring care and support for the rest of his life, possibly in a persistent vegetative state.'* I also refer to Lieutenant Colonel Brooks's report in which he also confirms that the 32-minute delay made no real difference to Mark's chances of survival.

Bowman Radio

This is a particularly significant area as it is partly the reason why Mark was in the position he was when he was shot. It is clear from the evidence that he was in that position partly because he wanted to get 'eyes on' and partly because he was trying to get signals on his radio. It was for these reasons that he went to the entrance knowing he was exposed and taking a risk. He needed to talk to Lance Sergeant Peek and Company Command. This was an extremely brave thing to do. He was under constant fire. Mark must have known the risks he faced. We do not know if he was not receiving any signal on his radio or just that the reception was poor. I remind you that it is not the purpose of the inquest to enquire into whether Bowman is the appropriate radio for the British Army, nor to find out if the British Army have enough of these radios or if the ECM (Electronic Counter Measures) interfere with the Bowman radios. That is a political matter to be debated by Parliament. My concern is how or whether it impacted on Mark's death.

Captain Moukarzel's report showed that the Welsh Guards were experiencing problems in Afghanistan with radios. *(The Coroner then read out all of Captain Moukarzel's report.)*

If Mark had been sent out on patrol without a radio or with a broken radio, that would be a matter of great concern. We heard yesterday that one soldier said that ECM blocked the Bowman radio whilst other soldiers said that it did not. The others said that other things affected the Bowman, examples being the terrain or the weather. We know as a fact that the platoon was having trouble with the radios on the patrol. What we need to know is if Mark had a dud radio or whether he was just suffering temporary problems. I think it is safe to assume that Lt Evison would have checked his radio before going out on patrol. From what I have heard of him, I can't imagine he would have gone out without doing so. I am also sure that if he was taking a patrol out and whilst he was out he had significant radio problems, he would have not continued with the patrol. We have heard that he was using his radio during the 30 minutes before he was wounded. This came out of the evidence of the soldiers, the log book records and from Major Bettinson who says he received communications from Lt Evison at 8.28, 8.32, 8.35 and 8.38.

It is likely that Mark was shot at 08:42 or around that time. Guardsman Tucker then used his radio successfully a few minutes after he fell. Tucker spoke to Company Command without difficulty. Tucker said in his statement that he saw Guardsman James treating Lt Evison and that he picked up Lt Evison's radio and informed Company Command of the casualty. He said he also heard Lance Sergeant Peek requesting help over the radio to get the platoon out of the compounds. I therefore conclude from the evidence that it is more likely than not that Mark Evison's Bowman radio was working but had temporary problems with the signal and that was one of the reasons why Mark moved into the doorway of the compound.

We have heard that there were difficulties with Personal Role Radios. However, in the evidence that we have heard, there have been frequent references to speaking on the Personal Role Radios. I am not saying that they did not have problems from time to time, however, it would be wrong to say they had no communications, just that they were sometimes ineffective.

The patrol base could see what was happening and gave assistance during the evacuation. I have thought about whether it was appropriate for me to discuss the decision to go out on patrol. I do not believe it is appropriate for me to do so. This is an operational issue.

That is a brief summary of the evidence heard. I am now here to record my conclusions and to do so, I need to refer to the recent Supreme Court decision in *R (on the application of Smith) v Oxfordshire Assistant Deputy Coroner.* This should make clear what my powers are. In my view, the Supreme Court was not creating new law. It was a majority decision that reinforces what Coroners had thought was the law.

I quote Lord Phillips in paragraph 88 of the judgment, *'In conducting the inquest, the Coroner should certainly attempt to satisfy the requirements of an Article 2 investigation.'*

I quote Lord Rodger at paragraph 122 of the judgement, *'Any suggestion that the death of a soldier in combat conditions points to some breach by the United Kingdom of his*

Article 2 right to life is not only to mistake, but – much worse – to devalue, what our soldiers do. It is not just that their job involves being exposed to the risk of death or injury. That is true of many jobs, from steeplejacks to firemen, from test pilots to divers. Uniquely, the job of members of the armed forces involves them being deployed in situations where, as they well know, opposing forces will actually be making a determined effort, and using all of their resources, to kill or injure them. While steps can be taken, by training and by providing suitable armour, to give our troops some measure of protection against these hostile attacks, that protection can never be complete. Deaths and injuries are inevitable. Indeed it is precisely because, in combat, our troops are inevitably exposed to these great dangers that they deserve the admiration of the community. The long-established exemption from inheritance tax on the estates of those who die on active service is an acknowledgment of the fact that members of the armed forces can be called upon to risk death in this way in the defence of what the government perceives to be the national interest.'

Lord Rodger at paragraph 127 says, *'The coroner is not concerned with broad political decisions which may seem to have a bearing, and may indeed actually have a bearing, on what happened. This is clear from Nachova v Bulgaria (2005), where the Grand Chamber described "the essential purpose" of an Article 2 investigation as being "to secure the effective implementation of the domestic laws safeguarding the right to life and, in those cases involving state agents or bodies, to ensure their accountability for deaths occurring* under their responsibility". Once it is established, say, that a soldier died because a blast from a roadside bomb penetrated the armour-plating on his vehicle, it may well be inferred that he would not have died if the plating had been stronger. And that simple fact may be worth pointing out as a possible guide for the future. But questions, say, as to whether it would have been feasible to fit stronger protection, or as to why the particular vehicles were used in the operation or campaign, or as to why those vehicles, as opposed to vehicles with stronger protection, were originally purchased by the Ministry of Defence, or as to whether it would have been better to have more helicopters available etc., all raise issues which are essentially political rather than legal. That being so, a curious aspect of Counsel's submissions before this Court was the complete absence of any reference to Parliament as the forum in which such matters should be raised and debated and in which ministers should be held responsible. Of course, in consequence of pressure brought to bear by Parliament, the government might set up an independent inquiry with wide terms of reference to look into all aspects of a situation, including the political aspects. But we are concerned with the scope of a coroner's inquest whose function is different. Many of the issues about the deaths of soldiers which are, understandably, of the greatest concern to their relatives are indeed of this much broader nature. In short, they raise questions of policy, not of legality, and so would fall outside the scope of any Article 2 investigation which a coroner might be obliged to carry out.'

I have told you that I have carried out an Article 2

investigation. The focus must be and has been on Mark. My concern as Coroner is not what medical supplies troops should carry or if they had whether it would have saved his life, it is not that the British Army should pledge to extract men who have been injured within what has been described as the 'golden hour'. My concern is should Mark have got to an operating theatre quickly, would it have saved his life. My concern is not with Bowman radios' compatibility with ECM. It is whether Mark had a Bowman radio and whether it was working as well as can be expected. The other things are political decisions to be decided by Parliament. I am quite sure if the government set up a public inquiry, I would be very surprised if they turned to me to comment on those issues.

I take on board what Mr Temple QC said yesterday that Mrs Evison is less than completely satisfied with the inquest. I hope you will give me credit that I have carried out a full investigation into the identity of the deceased, how and by what means he came by his death.

I record that Mark Lawrence Evison was born in London on 17 July 1982 and certified dead in Selly Oak Hospital, Birmingham on 12 May 2009. The injuries that caused his death were:

(1)(a) hypoxic brain injury due to

(1)(b) haemorrhagic shock due to

(1)(c) a gunshot wound to the right shoulder.

Verdict Lt Mark Lawrence Evison was killed by the enemy whilst on active service for our country.